ROUGH PASSAGE TO THE BODHI TREE

Praise for *Rough Passage to the Bodhi Tree*:

'*Rough Passage to the Bodhi Tree* presents a vivid, evocative fable of the Buddha's life, with a strong spiritual element and wisdom to it. Shiv Kumar has made Buddha's complex philosophies, especially of compassion and good action, deeply accessible'—Bapsi Sidhwa

'An imaginative recreation of the Buddha as a messiah of love, peace and compassion. A beautifully written story full of drama, suspense and romance'—Sharad Dutt, former director of Doordarshan

'This is a novel based on the life of the Buddha, written in a language that is evocative and charged with poetic intensity'
—B. Gopal Rao, critic and writer

Praise for *Nude before God*:

'A most amusing novel on a daring subject'—Graham Greene

'Very funny and clever and rather amusing . . . A modernist and emancipated writer, dealing with his native traditions rather fluently'—Christopher Hitchens

'The afterlife as satire. This heroic reissue resurrects a lost Indian classic'—Jeet Thayil

Praise for *Train to Delhi:*

'Shiv K. Kumar's novel has both beauty and power. It re-creates, in a language that glows with fragrance and colour, not only the trauma that one associates with Partition, but also love, compassion and forgiveness that it evoked even in the midst of communal frenzy. Here is a poet's visualization of the India of 1947—its brutality and romance, its agony and ecstasy'—Mulk Raj Anand

ROUGH PASSAGE TO THE BODHI TREE

SHIV K. KUMAR

PENGUIN BOOKS
An imprint of Penguin Random House

PENGUIN BOOKS

USA | Canada | UK | Ireland | Australia
New Zealand | India | South Africa | China | Singapore

Penguin Books is an imprint of the Penguin Random House group of companies whose addresses can be found at global.penguinrandomhouse.com

Published by Penguin Random House India Pvt. Ltd
4th Floor, Capital Tower 1, MG Road,
Gurugram 122 002, Haryana, India

Penguin
Random House
India

Published by Random House India in 2013

10 9 8 7 6 5 4 3 2

ISBN 9788184004502

Typeset in Minion Pro by R. Ajith Kumar

Printed at Repro India Limited

www.penguin.co.in

FSC
www.fsc.org
MIX
Paper from
responsible sources
FSC® C047271

This is a legitimate digitally printed version of the book and therefore might not have certain extra finishing on the cover.

To
Ramesh my son, not my son-in-law,
Vandana, my daughter,
Shehan, my grandson

BY THE SAME AUTHOR

The Best of Faiz

Nude before God

Train to Delhi

Liberation from pain is possible
through detachment.

…

Not through dogma or ritualism can salvation be
attained but only through
righteous action.

…

When I'm gone, let my teaching alone be
my successor.

The Buddha

1

King Suddhodana was pleasantly surprised when his son, Siddhartha, offered to take part in an open competition to win the hand of Princess Yashodhara. The royal chief priest, Asita, had advised the king that the only way to divert his son from his otherworldliness was to trap him in wedlock. The king had been worried about Siddhartha's spending long hours in meditation, and showing no interest in state affairs. Although the prince had received some training in martial arts, his heart lay in prayer and meditation. No wonder, he was called 'a brooding dove' by some.

Since King Suddhodana knew that his son would fare poorly in any martial competition, he thought of an arranged marriage for him. But Yashodhara's father, King Suprabuddha, insisted on honouring the Sakya tradition of an open contest to decide who would win his daughter's hand.

'But when your daughter is already in love with Siddhartha, where's the need to have a public display of martial skills?' asked Suddhodana.

'I'm afraid I cannot forsake the Sakya custom,' countered Suprabuddha.

When word went around about an open competition, which carried the fanfare of a swayamvara, three contestants jumped into the fray to win the hand of the most beautiful maiden in the kingdom. With anxiety and eagerness writ large across their faces, they waited breathlessly for the first round of the contest.

Yashodhara appeared on the scene, like a goddess on earth. Her complexion white as Nandini's milk, eyes glowing like starlight, she walked as gracefully into the ladies' enclosure as a gazelle.

One of the contestants was Devadatta, who'd never forgotten his humiliation at the hands of Siddhartha, his cousin. One morning, as they were both watching a flock of swans in the sky, Devadatta picked up his bow and shot down a swan which dropped on the ground, grievously wounded. Siddhartha rushed to the bird that was bleeding and gasping for breath, placed it on his lap, and wiped off the blood with a piece of cloth torn from his robe. Then he poured some water down its throat and caressed its feathers. The bird felt rejuvenated. When Devadatta claimed it as his prize, Siddhartha refused to surrender it. As an argument developed between the two, the matter was referred to Sage Kanya who decided in favour of Siddhartha.

'While you are its killer, O Devadatta,' the sage said, 'Siddhartha is its saviour. So you cannot claim the bird.'

Devadatta, therefore, took the contest as an opportunity to avenge this humiliation.

The other two contestants, Nanda and Arjuna, were also determined to vanquish Siddhartha, the crown prince of Kapilavastu. They hoped that he might even withdraw from the contest, 'brooding dove' that he was.

But to everyone's surprise, Siddhartha rode into the arena, on his milk-white horse, Kanaka, who neighed at the crowd, wondering what the occasion was all about. As Yashodhara caught a glimpse of the prince, she blushed. What if some other suitor won the day? she asked herself. She'd then immolate herself. As Siddhartha let Kanaka ride past the enclosure where Yashodara was seated, he stole a glance at her and smiled, as if assuring her that he'd certainly carry the day.

The first martial feat was the sword-play. Each contestant was required to cut the massive trunk of a mango tree at one stroke. Brandishing his sword, Devadatta leapt forward as if nothing could resist the sharp blade of his sword, not even a granite rock. But as he held up his sword and struck at the tree's trunk, its blade broke into splinters. Humiliated, he retreated to his seat.

Then Arjuna, whose mighty sword appeared invincible,

entered the arena. But as he plunged it into the trunk, it also splintered, and he too withdrew, his head bowed.

Nanda met the same fate, although he did a little better as his sword sliced the trunk more than halfway.

All eyes were now riveted on Siddhartha who stepped forward, holding in his right hand a bejewelled sword which glimmered in the mid-day sun. He first closed his eyes, as if he were muttering some mantra, and then kissed his sword's hilt. Then he plunged it into the trunk. So smoothly did the sword cleave through the trunk that the mango tree still stood erect, like a chicken whose head had been chopped off but whose body stood upright for a few seconds. Suddenly, the stout tree lurched to one side, and crashed to the ground. The crowd was stunned, and then a loud cheer rent the air.

When it came to archery, Arjuna whispered into Nanda's ears, 'That was the farthest Siddhartha can go. Maybe his sword had a special blade. So it was the steel that did it, not his might.' He paused. 'Now let me show you how my bow can sing as I twang it. And since my arrow has the eagle-eye, it can hit a target even if it moves like a shooting star.'

The target was a small cowry shell placed on a rock, fifteen *gows* away. It was multi-tinted, with a black dot on its centre. Each archer was required to hit the dot, not the outer shell of the cowry.

Arjuna was a renowned sharp-shooter who'd won many contests. He strutted forth, brandishing his bow above his head. It was a weapon that had never let him down so far. He steadied himself and then, concentrating on the black dot, he released the arrow. But it grazed past only the upper fringe of the cowry. He was knocked out of the contest.

He was followed by Nanda whose arrow hit only the rock on which the cowry stood. He, too, returned to his seat, defeated.

Devadatta also had to bite the dust as his arrow flew well beyond the cowry.

Next came Siddhartha, holding his bow which had a ruby-studded hilt. Holding it in his right hand, he pulled an arrow from his quiver and fixed it to the bow. Again he closed his eyes, and remained still for quite a while.

'There's the brooding dove,' bantered Arjuna to Nanda. 'Archery is not meditation, you know.'

'I agree,' responded Nanda.

Suddenly, the crowd erupted in a thunderous applause. Siddhartha's arrow had penetrated the black dot of the cowry.

'Well done!' shouted someone from the crowd.

'A neat stroke!' cried another man.

Yashodhara clapped her hands, her face radiant with joy. Sitting on the dais, King Suddhodana couldn't control his happiness. Turning to King Suprabuddha, he said, 'If he has come through so far, I'm sure he'll clear the last test as well.'

'I hope so,' Suprabuddha said. 'But it's always the last battle that decides a war.'

The final test, in horsemanship, turned out to be the toughest. Instead of riding his own steed, each competitor was required to mount an unbridled, savage stallion. So when a wild horse was brought into the arena, everyone in the audience was concerned about Siddhartha.

It was an ebony-coloured stallion, its nostrils breathing fire and its hooves digging into the ground. Glowering at the crowd, it seemed to challenge anyone to dare to come near it. Since mounting such a wild creature was like courting death, King Suddhodana was seized with fear. He summoned one of his counsellors to bring Siddhartha to him. As the prince approached the dais, the king whispered into his ears.

'No, my son, you are not going to risk your life. That stallion looks like Yama, out to kill anyone who touches it . . .' He paused. 'I don't care if this marriage doesn't come through . . .'

'But I'm committed to seeing it all through,' responded Siddhartha. 'It would be disgraceful if I threw up my hands now. You just pray for me, Father—that's all.' Siddhartha then walked back to his seat.

With fear lurking in his heart, Nanda rose to try his luck with this terrible beast. But as he drew close to it, it gave out a snort and charged at him like a wild boar. Nanda was kicked off his feet. There he now lay on the ground, squirming and bleeding. Although someone from the crowd shouted 'Oh God!' nobody had the courage to enter the arena and carry him away.

Arjuna had watched the spectacle with great trepidation. But since he was committed to participating in the contest, he rose to confront the horse. Strategically, he decided to go around the stallion to look for a vantage point from where to mount it. He hoped that if he approached it from the rear, he would be able to take the animal by surprise. But since the stallion had already seen him entering the arena, it turned around, breathing fire from its dilated nostrils, and attacked Arjuna, who lost his nerve and bolted away.

It was now Devadatta's turn to prove his mettle. Learning from Nanda's attempt, he rushed into the arena when the stallion was looking elsewhere, so before it could turn around, he had already jumped onto it. Glowing with pride, he raised his right hand and waved to the crowd. But he'd hardly settled on the stallion's back when it began to leap up and down. So wild and unsettling were the jerks that Devadatta realized that he could be thrown off at any moment. Suddenly, the stallion rose on its hind legs, and the next moment Devadatta found himself writhing on the ground. The game was up for him too.

All eyes now turned to Siddhartha, who gathered himself to his feet, looking resolute and composed. But before he could step into the arena, King Suddhodana stepped down from the dais and implored his son, 'No, Siddhartha, hold back—for my sake!'

But Siddhartha responded, 'Don't worry, Father, I won't

let you down . . . I have already requested you to just pray for me.'

Dejected, the king returned to his seat on the dais. But now he sat with his eyes closed and his head cupped in his hands.

In the ladies' enclosure, Yashodhara looked frightened, her face sallow, hands quaking and heart pounding. A hush had fallen all over the place—not a stir anywhere, not a whisper.

Siddhartha was now seen walking slowly into the arena, his eyes shining with some divine light. Before the stallion could start snorting and digging its hooves into the ground, Siddhartha's right hand was already on its mane. Gently, his fingers began to caress its neck and flanks. Then two pairs of eyes met as if they were communicating with each other in some strange language. As he now moved to the other side, the stallion also looked around to ensure that he was still there. It seemed as if the animal had been bewitched by Siddhartha's love and compassion.

Gently, Siddhartha mounted the stallion and kissed its head. He was now riding it in circles—from the ladies' enclosure where Yashodhara sat, to the dais where King Suddhodana almost cried out with joy. It was only when Siddhartha stopped the stallion near the dais that the king realized it was not a fantasy. Then King Suprabuddha rose to his feet, raising his hands as a gesture of blessing for the winner.

As Siddhartha dismounted from the stallion, a loud applause reverberated in the air. Yashodhara rushed to Siddhartha, put a garland of mogra flowers round his neck, and knelt to touch his feet.

'I'm yours, O Siddhartha,' she said, tears of joy streaming down her cheeks.

2

Now that Siddhartha had won his bride in an open competition, there was a flurry of activities on both sides. While Yashodhara's parents brought diamonds, rubies and brocaded robes for Siddhartha, King Suddhodana gifted a separate palace to the couple. Then the priests from both sides consulted each other to agree upon an auspicious day for the wedding.

A week before the ceremony, Kapilavastu was agog with festivities—singing, dancing and feasting. While the bride's friends sang doleful songs about her parting from her parents, Yashodhara looked forward to living with Siddhartha. She kept thinking about his martial prowess—his taming of the wild stallion, his superb skill at archery and his sword-play. But, above all, she yearned for the wedding night. Would he vanquish her in bed just as he'd tamed the wild stallion? Then she saw herself as the wife of the crown prince of Kapilavastu, with a retinue of maid-servants at her beck and call.

But destiny crashed into her dreams when she heard, just a day before the wedding, that King Ballamaya, of the neighbouring state of Gagana, had launched a surprise attack on Kapilavastu. The enemy torched houses, devastated the paddy fields near the border, and killed several Sakya soldiers. Someone brought word that the attack was launched at the insistence of Devadatta who was a close friend of the enemy's commander-in-chief. It was obvious that he wanted to avenge his humiliation at the open competition.

Although Kapilavastu was taken by surprise, King Suddhodana did not lose any time in mobilizing his forces to meet the challenge. While he positioned himself at the head of his army, a division of crack soldiers was dispatched to the border to drive the enemy away.

The king asked Siddhartha to stay away from the battlefield, but the prince decided to plunge into the fray, for wasn't he the prime cause of Ballamaya's invasion? He would like to confront Devadatta on the battlefield, unless he chose to direct the operation clandestinely.

When Channa, Siddhartha's charioteer, brought the chariot right up to the battlefront, the king glowered at his son.

'Why are you here to risk your life, my son?'

'If there is a time to meditate under a tree, there's also a time to fight for a worthy cause. I know that the real enemy on the other side is not King Ballamaya but Devadatta.'

The king then directed a company of skilled soldiers to guard his son.

Surprisingly, Siddhartha didn't use his bow and arrows for quite a while. He just stood in his chariot, reclining against its flagstaff, watching the dance of death on both sides. 'Why involve helpless animals, horses and elephants, in the battle?' he asked Channa.

Smiling, his charioteer responded, 'Why don't you ask Kanaka? Maybe he understands all this better than you or myself.'

Siddhartha turned towards Kanaka, caressed his mane, let his fingers run all over his flanks, and then looked deep into his eyes. 'Yes, dear friend, what do you have to say?'

The horse just gave out a gentle snort and started licking Siddhartha's hands.

'I think,' Siddhartha said to Channa, 'he is saying "I know it all but I wouldn't speak out." So, you see, an animal doesn't articulate, it speaks only through silence and gestures.'

After a pause, he resumed. 'O Channa, here's another spectacle of suffering, much more gruesome than what we saw in the marketplace a few months ago—soldiers and animals lying in pools of blood.'

Suddenly, a rider reined in his horse to the left of Siddhartha's chariot.

'O Prince, I have a message for you,' he said.

'What message, and from whom?'

'From Princess Yashodhara. She wants you to take care of yourself . . . She is praying for your well-being.'

Deeply touched, the prince responded, 'Tell her that if I am armed with her prayers, how can any harm come my way?'

As Siddhartha was standing in the chariot watching the battle, an arrow grazed past his left ear. Immediately, he ducked to save himself. But noticing how he'd exposed himself to danger, Channa turned to him. 'O Prince, why are you risking your life? Don't you realize that you are on a battlefield, not meditating under some tree?'

'I know, Channa . . . I'll take care of myself. But meditation can be done anywhere, any time—fighting an enemy, riding a horse, talking or eating . . .'

'But, please, don't do it here when arrows are flying thick and fast in the air.'

Siddhartha smiled. 'But tell me, Channa, don't you feel scared yourself, steering my chariot through this battlefield, weaponless?'

'No,' he responded, 'because I feel like Lord Krishna, charioteer to Arjuna.'

Word now came from the front that the enemy had started to retreat, overpowered by the Sakya soldiers. Then King Suddhodana saw his commander-in-chief bringing back King Ballamaya, who looked pale and helpless, in his chariot.

'Shall I give the order for him to be beheaded right here?' asked his commander-in-chief.

'Let me do it myself,' replied King Suddhodana, unsheathing his sword.

'No, Father,' came a voice from the chariot just behind. 'Why kill someone who is already half dead? Let us vanquish him with a still more lethal weapon than the sword—compassion and forgiveness.'

'So the brooding dove is back into spirituality,' said the king, surprised. 'Do you realize how many soldiers and animals we have lost in this battle?'

'I have seen it all, Father,' said Siddhartha. 'But vengeance is no way to punish an enemy . . . I plead on his behalf.'

Before King Suddhodana could say anything more, Ballamaya stepped towards the prince and bowed to touch his feet.

'No, King Ballamaya, a king should never bow to another king, and least of all to a prince,' said Siddhartha.

Overwhelmed, Ballamaya said to Siddhartha, 'This is the stuff divinity is made of.' He paused. 'But let me confess that this invasion was not my doing.'

'Then who instigated you?' asked Siddhartha.

'Devadatta,' came the prompt answer.

'It's a pity that his evil design didn't work,' said Siddhartha. 'Still, please, convey my good wishes to him. After all, he's my cousin.'

'I've never met anyone like you,' said Ballamaya. Then,

turning to King Suddhodana, he added, 'I'll always remain a captive in the hands of your son, held by the magnanimity of his soul. Let me now take a vow that I'll remain at your service any time, anywhere.'

'Let him be released and sent back, unharmed,' announced King Suddhodana, 'as this is my son's wish.'

Bowing to both father and son, King Ballamaya walked away, saying, 'God bless you both!'

Far away, in the palace of King Suprabuddha, a hot argument was going on between father and daughter.

'I am very sad to say that you didn't care to send your troops in support of King Suddhodana,' said Yashodhara.

'These are state matters,' retorted her father, 'in which you need not interfere. I didn't wish to fight against Ballamaya who has done no harm to me.'

'But didn't he launch an unprovoked attack on your would-be son-in-law's territory?'

'Don't talk too much,' snapped Suprabuddha. 'You are not married to him, yet.'

'Love doesn't lean on rituals, Father,' she said. 'It's a relationship that transcends the bond solemnized by priests.' She paused. 'Even if this marriage doesn't come through, I will always look upon him as my husband.'

These words stunned King Suprabuddha and he said, 'I'm sorry. I'll immediately order my soldiers to join King Suddhodana's army to defend Kapilavastu.'

'Too late now, dear Father,' she said. 'I've just received a message that King Ballamaya has surrendered. But when he was about to be beheaded, Siddhartha entreated his father to forgive him and let him go unharmed.'

'Then why don't you forgive me too?' asked Suprabuddha.

'I do, dear Father,' she replied. 'That was just a little wrangle between father and daughter.' She paused. 'I love you too.'

'As much as you love Siddhartha?' he asked, smiling.

'While he's the entire world to me, you, my creator, have all my respect.'

As the dust of the battle settled down, the priests from both sides consulted each other again and agreed upon another auspicious day for the wedding. Kapilavastu now returned to its festive mood.

As for Siddhartha, he felt as if he had been tossed from one end of a see-saw to another—from the battlefield to the wedding ceremony. Yashodhara however, was lost in her dreams.

3

It was an exhausting day for Siddhartha. While he kept brooding over what the future might hold for him, Yashodhara remained in a state of bliss. She was to be married to a prince, young and handsome, with a generous heart. There he was—his long, black curly hair falling over his shoulders, eyes glowing bright, and his body shapely as if sculpted in marble. But why did he look so tense, she wondered.

Winter came early to Kapilavastu that year. Even in the first week of September, mist began to form everywhere, veiling the sunrise, so that most vehicles had to remain off the streets till noon. But in spite of the biting chill, a large crowd of poor people had gathered at the palace gates to receive offerings of food and clothing from the royal household.

Wedding rituals began at dawn in the audience hall of

the palace. At the centre was a havan-kund around which sat six priests—bare-chested, with sacred threads dangling around their necks—chanting slokas from the Vedas. While on one side of the havan-kund sat King Suddhodana, on the other side sat Siddhartha and Yashodhara. The entire hall exuded the fragrance of the sacred fire.

After the chanting had run for a short while, the High Priest asked Siddhartha to hold a lump of camphor in a large spoon, light it and then drop it on a pile of mango wood in the havan-kund. Flames now leapt into the air, like a brood of snakes let loose from a snake-charmer's basket. Thereafter, both the bride and the bridegroom kept pouring into the fire spoonfuls of ghee and samagri, whenever the priests chanted 'swaha'.

Then came the moment when Siddhartha and Yashodhara were asked to stand up and walk around the fire seven times. As she followed Siddhartha, she looked like an apsara who had descended from *indraloka* to wed an earthling.

Although she wore jewels and gems of all kinds, it was an emerald necklace that she held close to her heart, because it was a gift she had received from Siddhartha when they first met. In her eyes was the sparkle of a dream—her first night with someone who, she knew, would transport her into *ekstasis*.

The wedding rituals continued till late in the afternoon. It was only in the evening that the High Priest asked the couple to hold each other's hands, and recite after him the gayatri mantra, eleven times. Then he declared them both husband and wife, wishing them love, peace and glory.

Instantly, the hall erupted into cheer. Everyone rushed forward to bless the couple, showering them with yellow rice or petals of roses.

Ceremony over, the newly-weds were escorted by the High Priest to a decorated chariot, waiting outside the hall. There was Channa, holding the reins of Kanaka, 'Please accept my good wishes too, O Prince,' he said. Looking at them both, he exclaimed, 'The handsomest couple in Kapilavastu!'

'Thank you, Channa,' responded Siddhartha. Then, turning to Yashodhara, he said, 'This is Channa, not just my charioteer, but also my friend and confidant.'

Channa blushed at the compliment.

'This is the magnanimity of his heart,' Channa said to Yashodhara. 'You know, he sometimes calls me his Sanjaya, but he is not blind like King Dhritarashtra in the Mahabharata. He has seen enough, understood everything . . .'

Realizing the special bond of respect and affection between the two, Yashodhara took a ruby ring from her left hand, and said, 'A small gift for you, Channa.'

Overwhelmed by her gesture, he stuttered, 'This is too much.'

'Nothing is too much when hearts are bound in affection,' she said. 'Hereafter, we'll be the three of us, not just two . . . I look forward to hearing more about you from my husband.'

Channa then drove the chariot to a separate wing of the palace gifted by the king to his son and daughter-in-law.

It was a luxuriously furnished palace—velvet carpets on the floors, magnificent paintings on the walls, and gold-threaded curtains hanging on the windows. But the most gorgeous room in the palace was the bed-chamber for the newly-weds. In the middle of this room was a large rosewood bed, over which hung an embroidered silken canopy. On the bed was a thistledown mattress with two filigreed pillows. A heavenly nuptial bed, it was designed only for some god and his consort.

While Yashodhara waited in excitement, Siddhartha was lost in thought. On his face was an otherworldly look as if his eyes were hitched to some remote star in the sky. Yashodhara noticed this, but she was certain that he would soon come to her, fully charged with intense desire.

She undressed herself, taking off all her jewellery, except the emerald necklace. Anticipating a cold night, King Suddhodana had thoughtfully arranged a logwood fire in a corner of the room.

Lying cosily under the covers, Yashodhara waited for Siddhartha to join her—this was the moment she had dreamt of all through the rituals. On the lawns outside, the royal musicians were playing on their instruments, with the razzle-dazzle of the wedding lights illuminating the entire firmament. It was a befitting backdrop for a royal couple about to savour love.

Surprisingly, Siddhartha seemed to be miles away, lost to another world. He was pacing up and down the room, from the bed to a window and back, like a tiger in a cage.

'What's come over you, darling?' Her voice rose from under the covers. 'Why have you gone so quiet? Not a word spoken . . . and here I am in bed, waiting for you.'

'I'll be there . . .' he mumbled. But he didn't stop in his tracks.

'It's our wedding night, darling.' There was gentle pleading in her voice. 'Here I am, under the covers, with nothing on my body except your emerald necklace. But it lies frigid and heavy on my breasts. I am feeling cold and lonesome. Even the logwood fire . . .' she trailed off.

She now saw him stop at the window for a while, looking outside. Impatiently, she sat up in bed, reclining against the silken pillows. Then she spoke, this time with a ring of petulance in her voice. 'What are you seeing out there?'

He turned around for a moment and mumbled, 'I was just thinking . . .'

But she intervened, saying, 'This is not the time for thinking. It's for doing . . . you know what I mean.' She paused. 'In any case, out there it's just the glow of the wedding lights, and the blaring music.'

'I know,' he said. 'But I wonder what lies beyond those lights. Darkness, I suppose. Those grey zones of the unknown, that mystery of some uncharted territory.' Then, looking directly at Yashodhara, he asked, 'Have you ever seen a dark, hollow space within a candle's flame? Right at its centre resides peace, amidst agitation. Why is the heart of darkness so tranquil, its soul so calm and secure?'

'I don't know what you are talking about,' she said. 'What about the dark spaces in my heart, the muffled voice of my loneliness? You are talking about the soul of darkness and its tranquillity, but what about the body? Where would the soul reside if it didn't have warm, protective vesture?' With a deep sigh, she added, 'I wish I could ask the musicians to stop playing. Their loud noise seems to shatter the peace in this room.'

'I agree that noise is always invasive. But, what about the silence that follows, like the darkness beyond any razzle-dazzle? Doesn't life revolve around contraries? There is the still centre of the axle within the outer circumference of a wheel . . .'

'Look, dear Siddha,' she burst out, 'I don't understand all this . . . I feel like jumping out of the bed to drag you into it. Why have you forgotten that this is our wedding night?'

'I plead guilty, my love—very guilty,' he said. 'But I feel that even on our wedding night, we should be candid with each other. I have always prized candour and transparency above everything else. For instance, when Channa was driving us after the rituals, I couldn't help recalling what I'd seen, some time ago, in the marketplace of Kapilavastu. Yasho, I then encountered for the first time, sickness, old age and death. Those gruesome images still haunt me—that hungry man, holding out his bowl for food . . .'

'What about the appetite of the body, the lips that yearn for the nectar of a kiss?' She paused. 'I wish you'd also seen that day in the marketplace, a wedding procession—the face of a bride, peeping out of her palanquin, telling the world that she was on her way to marital bliss. Remember, that there is always a moment to forget all sorrows of life to capture joy and happiness when one can . . . Let me say that if you were recalling those painful images, I too carry in my mind a fond memory of a handsome prince taming a wild, unbridled stallion.' She paused. 'How did you tame that horse, Siddha?'

'Well, I understood that what that savage creature needed was compassion and understanding,' he responded. 'So I just walked up to it, looked into its eyes, caressed its brown, glossy mane, its muzzle, kissed its head—and there it was, ready to let me ride it without resisting.'

Yashodhara seized the moment and said, smiling, 'I am also waiting to be bridled, because every bride on her wedding night yearns to be tamed, her body's appetite satiated, her thirst quenched . . .'

'I give in to you, my love,' he said. 'No more talking . . . I'll be there with you.'

He then walked slowly towards the bed, like someone sleepwalking.

4

In bed, she took over. While Siddhartha lay under her, almost immobile, she rode high like an unbridled, wild stallion. Eyes flaming with passion, hair flying like the mane of a stallion in full gallop, she seemed to be a woman possessed. Impetuously, she kissed him all over—his forehead, eyes, lips, chest, thighs and legs, as if she were anointing some deity for a ritual.

'I think I must now take off even my emerald necklace,' she breathed into his ears, 'because it's coming in the way.' She felt a lump in her throat. 'Isn't making love like entering an uncharted territory?'

While Yashodhara was up in the clouds, beyond even the moon and stars, he felt as if he were called upon by destiny to do his duty.

'Why don't you also move?' she pleaded. 'I love you,

Siddha, more than you can imagine. I think I was born only for this moment.'

Out of compassion for her, he now put his arms around her, pressing her fervently to his bosom.

'I love you too, Yasho,' he murmured.

'At this moment,' she said, in a voice gentle and plaintive, 'I feel like a hungry beggar with a bowl . . . won't you drop something into it?'

'What do you want, my love?' he said, tenderly.

'A son!' she exclaimed, as if she were asking a boon of some god.

'Maybe,' he said, smiling.

'But I'd like him to grow into a full-blooded young man—open, and not close-fisted like you,' she teased him. 'I hope you are not annoyed with me for saying this. Of course, now you have come along with me. I am beholden to you.'

'Well,' he said pensively, 'since he'd be my creation too, how can I guarantee that he wouldn't also be a brooding dove?' Smiling, he planted a gentle kiss on her lips.

'Whether a brooding dove, or an unbridled stallion, I'll take him as a gift from you. But I also know that he'd be as handsome as my Siddha. And he'd stay with me whenever you are away, riding with Channa.'

It was well beyond midnight. Since there were now no lights, and the royal musicians had stopped playing, darkness and silence descended over the palace. Only a shaft of moonlight lay across the floor of the bedroom, with the dying embers of the logwood fire.

Lying alongside her husband, Yashodhara sank into deep sleep, all passion spent. She looked like a devotee dozing off on the floor of a temple, exhausted after ringing bells and chanting mantras.

But Siddhartha was awake, his eyes focused on the ceiling where he noticed an insect crawling towards a cornice. Do insects sleep at night? he wondered. And what about a fish that swims in a river day and night—are its eyes open? Since a fish has a mind too, it must be thinking something all the time. He recalled how Asita, the royal priest, had once told him that the fish was God's first creation.

Siddhartha turned towards Yashodhara and saw that she was fast asleep. He noticed a couple of tears on her left cheek. Were these tears of love's consummation, or a manifestation of some inner frustration? he wondered.

Sleep eluded him that night. Assuming that Yashodhara wouldn't awaken till late in the morning, he crept out of bed to go for a stroll on the lawn outside. He'd often done this at dawn. The moisture of dew-drops under his feet always made him feel close to earth. What was the secret behind creation? he often mused. Why had animals and birds been denied the faculty of speech, while man discoursed, argued and wrangled? Was marriage only for procreation? Didn't lust enter into every act of love?

As the grey of dawn started brightening into orange, and

then crimson, he suddenly thought of going to Channa, even though he wasn't sure if he'd be up at that time.

Walking over to his cottage, which was near the eastern gate of the main palace, he knocked at the door. It was Channa's wife who answered it. Surprised, she ran inside to inform her husband that it was Prince Siddhartha at the door.

'At this hour, O Prince?' Channa stuttered, rubbing sleep out of his eyes.

'I'm sorry to disturb you so early,' said Siddhartha. 'But something surged within me . . .'

'Always a pleasure to meet you, O Master—anywhere, any time.'

'I have come here at this odd hour, not as your master but your friend.'

'In any case, I was about to get up myself,' Channa said. 'Come inside, please . . . Every morning, I massage my little daughter's feet and legs. She won't let her mother do it.' Then he explained that Saroja was a cripple.

As Siddhartha looked at the child in bed, her legs swollen and twisted, he said, 'You never told me about her . . .'

'You have already seen enough suffering, O Prince,' he said. Then, gesturing to him reverently to sit on a cot, he said, 'But wasn't this your wedding night?'

'Yes, Channa . . . but a compulsive urge has brought me to you . . . let me tell you that I didn't have any sleep last night. I kept musing all the time.'

'You must try to get over your brooding, somehow. I'm afraid it may be your undoing some day.'

'My undoing, or my salvation?' Siddhartha quipped.

There was a brief silence.

'All right, what's the matter?' Channa asked. 'Is there anything I can do for you?'

'Let me share with you what's agitating me . . . There's nobody else I can turn to.' Then, bluntly he asked, 'Channa, should I have got married?'

'Marriage is sacrosanct. How would the world move on otherwise? Even Lord Krishna was married. In fact, he had two women in his life, his wife Rukmani and Radha, his beloved. What about Lord Shiva and his consort Parvati? I'm sure sage Vishwamitra would have married Menaka after he fell in love with her . . .'

Siddhartha smiled, his eyes lingering on Channa's face. 'I'm indeed impressed by your learning. I take you as someone who is wiser than even Asita, or any of my father's counsellors.'

Blushing at this compliment, Channa said, 'All this I got from my grandmother who used to tell me stories.'

'Still, you have cited examples which don't hold much water in my case. While Krishna and Shiva were gods, and Vishwamitra was a blessed sage, I'm just a mortal . . .'

'Mortal, O Prince?' Channa said, smiling. 'Don't you know what Asita has predicted about you—that you'll some day be the King of kings?'

'I think he was imagining it. Who can predict the future? It's that grey zone of mystery that nobody can penetrate . . . Channa, what's the genesis of pain?'

This sudden question almost knocked Channa off.

'This falls far beyond me, O Prince . . . you should go and ask Asita.'

'Well, I'll try him out . . .'

Siddhartha got up. 'I must go back to my bedroom in case Yashodhara sends someone to track me down . . . I do feel relieved after talking to you.'

As he was walking back to his palace, the sun appeared above the horizon. It looked like a golden eye just woken after a night's rest. Was there also a hollow, dark spot at the heart of this ball of fire? he wondered.

Right at the door of his bedroom, Yashodhara was standing, looking awfully worried.

'Where had you gone so early in the morning?' she asked.

'I should have told you that I always go out in the morning to watch the sunrise, not that I am a sun-worshipper.'

Looking somewhat mystified, she said, 'But you could have watched the sunrise from that window, it could be your portal to the world outside.'

'No, the sun would look a prisoner through the bars of a window,' he countered. 'It appears in its full glory only when seen from an open ground.'

'I'd never be able to match you, darling,' she said, looking adoringly at him. 'You should teach me to think and argue.'

'Then you'd have to spend a lot of time at that window.' He smiled. 'But alone, because it cannot accommodate two persons. Strait is the pathway to self-realization.'

'There you go again, philosophizing. But I love you all the more for it.' Then, drawing close to him, she said, 'Won't you kiss me?'

Holding her in a warm embrace, Siddhartha planted a gentle kiss on her lips. But there was in it more compassion and understanding than any emotional fervour.

'Thank you, my love,' Yashodhara said, beaming.

5

As suggested by Channa, Siddhartha decided to seek knowledge of life from Asita.

As he was walking towards his room, he learnt that he had been called by his father to the audience hall to assist him in deciding a legal dispute. So Siddhartha turned towards the audience hall, hoping to meet the High Priest there.

He noticed that the hall was fully packed. Since he was dressed in plain clothes, he sat in a corner, unrecognized by anyone. While th king sat on the dais, flanked by Asita and some counsellors, on the floor stood a petitioner, looking utterly distraught. On the opposite side was a young, beautiful woman, and a man standing just behind her. As the chief counsellor asked the petitioner to present his case, the man first bowed to the king and then began to speak.

'I am a cursed man, O King, absolutely devastated.'

Then, pointing towards the woman on the other side, he said, 'There stands my wife who has betrayed my trust. Outrageously, she has snapped the sacred bond of marriage which is sanctified by the gods.' Then, pointing an accusing finger at the man behind her, he added, 'And there stands my home-breaker, my wife's paramour. They are both rakshasas who should be awarded the severest punishment.'

A voice then rose from the dais. It was Asita. 'It is not for you to suggest what punishment should be awarded. That is the prerogative only of King Suddhodana. You may just place the pertinent facts before us.'

Upset by Asita's curt intervention, the man resumed. 'I apologize for being carried away by my emotions.' Clearing his throat, he said, 'I am a farmer and every day, from morning till evening, I am away tilling my paddy field, in rain or sunshine, heat or cold. One day, since there was a heavy downpour, I came home early. As I entered my house, I heard some voices in my bedroom. I went around to the rear side and peeped through a window.'

At this point, the farmer broke down in tears. Wiping his face with the back of his left hand, he resumed, 'There, in my bed, were my wife and that man, both undressed, making love. If I had a knife in my hand, I would have jumped through the window and killed them both. Why should my wife betray me when I have been faithful to her all my life? And there she now stands, a creature of lust.' Then, glowering at her paramour, he added, 'He is also a married man. I wonder if his wife knows the truth about her husband.'

As he stopped, a man from the front row shouted, 'Shame!' Someone from the rear said, 'She should be stripped and whipped.' Siddhartha then heard a man whispering into his neighbour's ears: 'Wouldn't it be exciting to see her disrobed—punishment for her but an exciting spectacle for us all?'

So it was carnal desire that excited most humans, thought Siddhartha.

The chief counsellor then asked the woman to make her statement.

'Do you wish to say anything in your defence, although it seems to be a prima facie case of wanton adultery?'

'No, sir,' the woman replied, in a voice that sounded anguished. 'I am not guilty. I am an innocent woman who was raped while my husband was away at work.'

A wave of shock swept through the audience. But it was her lover who looked shattered. It seemed as if the earth had given way under his feet. His eyes blazed like burning coals. He raised his right hand as if seeking permission to intervene. But the chief counsellor said, 'Patience! Wait for your turn.'

The woman was then asked to continue with her statement.

'I have been a dutiful wife to my husband whom I love and adore. Every evening, I wait for him, with a bowl of rice and a glass of hot milk. That afternoon, just as I had done my laundry, this man barged into my house, pushed me into the bed, and raped me. O noble King, can a woman protect herself from a rapist?'

For a moment, Siddhartha was confounded. Was she really innocent? he wondered. He saw some faces in the hall now looking angrily at the alleged rapist. A loud voice was heard, saying, 'Let him be flogged in the marketplace!'

As for the farmer, her husband, he stood dumbfounded. Had he accused his wife unjustly when the real culprit was the man standing behind her?

'I have nothing more to say, O noble King,' she said. 'I am unblemished. Even though this man has outraged my modesty, I claim to be chaste like a lotus, because my soul is pure.' She trailed off, wiping tears from her face.

A pall of silence descended on the audience hall. Siddhartha was caught on the horns of a dilemma. Eagerly, he awaited the verdict of his father.

Everyone was now anxious to hear the alleged rapist, whose face had gone ashen, and whose hands were shaking. When he was called upon to speak, he almost choked.

'O King, this woman is an evil creature. I don't know what to say. I falter and fumble for words.' Then, raising his hands up in the air, he said, 'If I don't get justice on this earth, the gods in heaven will certainly absolve me of all blame.' Then, turning towards the woman, he added, 'Fair may be her face, but dark as a raven is the soul that she claims to be pure as a lotus.' He paused momentarily as if unsure of what to say next. 'O gracious King,' he resumed, 'this woman is a seducer. Indeed, I plead guilty of letting myself fall into her trap. Even sages, like Vishwamitra, have not been able to resist a temptress.

'Let me add that it has not happened just once, but several times. Since I happen to be her neighbour, I was easily accessible to her. My wife is a seamstress who works for a tailor, three times a week. As there is only a low wall dividing our two houses, this woman could easily see my wife going out for work. Then, minutes later, she would jump over the wall and take me into my bedroom. That afternoon, a heavy downpour held my wife back at the tailor's shop. So, fearful of her returning home early, this woman asked me to come over to her own house—and that was the moment when we were both caught red-handed in the act itself. Weak man that I am, I always let myself be seduced by her. I should have realized that if caught, I'd cause unbearable pain to this innocent farmer. But before I conclude my statement, let me say that I marvel at this woman's ingenuity in turning around to call me a rapist, just to save her own skin. My heart bleeds for her husband.' He paused. Then, looking compassionately at the farmer, he said, 'Yes, I do plead guilty, and I'd cheerfully accept any punishment awarded to me.'

A wave of shock swept through the audience. 'Poor man!' someone cried out from the audience.

There were now consultations on the dais, between the king, Asita and the royal counsellors. Meanwhile, a hush had fallen all over the place. Even Siddhartha sat, eagerly awaiting the judgment.

Then Asita rose to pronounce the verdict on behalf of the king: 'Three years of solitary confinement for the farmer's wife, and a fortnight's prison for the seamstress's husband . . .'

What would all this lead to, Siddhartha wondered—loneliness for the farmer, and the arduous task of running his household. As for the seamstress's husband, there lay ahead of him the dread of estrangement from his wife, for she'd certainly come to know about his infidelity. A tangled web was human life. It was quite painful for Siddhartha to see the seamy side of human relationships. Since the day's experience had been an eye-opener, he decided to attend a few more sessions in the audience hall.

A fortnight later, it was a case of a land dispute between two brothers, each claiming a lion's share of their father's property. As each argued his case, it appeared as if they were now sworn enemies, poised to ruin each other. On another occasion, it was a domestic servant who had strangled his aged mistress and had run away with her jewellery.

There was now no need for him, he thought, to seek any more understanding of life from Asita, for he had already learnt that the genesis of human pain was desire—lust or greed. Would a bird grab another bird's nest, or would a horse seduce another horse's mare? Are birds hoarders like human beings? Do they have sacks of grains stacked away in some safe place? Do they have permanent nests, or do they spend a night in any tree, anywhere? And when a bird or animal dies, is there a cremation?

His visits to the audience hall pushed him still deeper into solitary contemplation. For hours, he'd sit under some tree and reflect on human conduct.

Whenever Yashodhara saw him lost in thought, pacing up and down the hallway of their palace, she was saddened. How should she pull him out of his depression?

Then, one day, she felt stirrings in her womb. That night, as they were lying in bed, she turned over to him and whispered, 'Darling, are you ready to hear some exciting news?'

'What's it, Yasho?' he asked.

'I think something is coming up . . . I'm going to be a mother.'

'That's happy news indeed,' he responded, although deep down in his heart he felt as if there'd now be another cog in the wheel of his life, another knot to tie him down to earth.

'There'll be no more loneliness for me,' Yashodhara said.

Siddhartha smiled.

'When he grows up, I'll have that window sealed,' she came on. 'No looking into the grey zones beyond light. It will be just light everywhere, day and night.'

Siddhartha beamed. He must empathize with the happiness of a mother-to-be, he told himself. So, glancing compassionately at her, he said, 'I'm glad you'll now have someone to fill up all the blank spaces in your heart.'

When she delivered a male child, there was exuberant jubilation all over Kapilavastu. King Suddhodana announced that there would be no hearings in the audience hall for a month, because they occasioned only tales of suffering. The royal kitchen was thrown open to all the poor people, and no Brahmin went away without a generous offering.

Asita acted as the High Priest at the naming ceremony of the new-born. After a long puja came the moment for him to announce the name.

'Since the name should begin with the letter "R",' said Asita, 'let him be called Rahul.'

A thunderous cheer rose in the air.

The next day, when Asita was asked to foretell the child's future, his brow darkened.

'What's the matter?' asked the king.

Looking at the child's face, and holding his horoscope in his right hand, he said, 'I'm afraid, this child will also follow in his father's footsteps. I've just noticed a crescent-shaped mark on his forehead, below a wisp of hair on the left side. This shows that he'll also be spiritual, like his father. Of course, his body doesn't carry the thirty-two sacred marks, like Siddhartha's. So he may not go as far as his father. In a sense, both your son and grandson have been lost to spirituality.'

Feeling perturbed, the king looked angrily at Asita.

'This is the second time you've shattered me with your ominous predictions. Eighteen years ago, you made two predictions—first, that Siddhartha would become motherless within seven days of his birth, and second, that he'd renounce the world. Unfortunately, your first prediction did come true and I lost my wife, Mahamaya, a few days after Siddhartha's birth. But God is great because I found a foster nurse, Princess Mahaprajapati, to breastfeed my child. She nursed him like his real mother, and loved him as dearly as her own son, Samir. I was glad to gift her a small palace on the royal grounds. A thousand pities, however, that she had to leave Kapilavastu when Siddhartha was about ten months old.

'But thereafter, he was brought up by the royal maids. So how did he suffer from motherlessness?' He took a deep breath and then resumed, 'As regards your other prediction that he'd renounce the world, don't you see him now a happily married man—and the father of a son?' Then with a sneer on his lips, he asked Asita, 'Has my Siddhartha renounced the world?'

'But this is not the end of the day, O King,' countered Asita. 'The future is a dark tunnel, with many unpredictable twists and turns. Maybe the next few days will tell which way the dice will turn.'

'Oh, your arrogance,' the king snapped. 'You priests act like gods; you gloat over your omniscience.'

'O King,' responded Asita, 'I always say what I see in a horoscope, whether it is Siddhartha's or your grandson's.'

'Maybe this time your soothsaying will fall apart.'

'I hope so too,' Asita said, 'because I wish you all happiness. But . . .' he broke off.

Sleep eluded the king that night, he was besieged by dark forebodings.

Next morning, when he told his chief counsellor that he felt like dismissing Asita, he was advised not to precipitate the matter.

'Let's not act rashly,' the counsellor said. 'On the contrary, you may ask him to perform some ritual to propitiate the gods. There must be some way to avert what he has predicted.'

When the king asked Asita if any propitiary rites could change the future, Asita said, 'What's written in the horoscope cannot be wiped off. Not even all your tears and prayers could alter a syllable written in the horoscope.'

The king still chose to ignore the prediction.

As Siddhartha attended some more sessions in the audience hall, he felt disillusioned with the world. He now realized that he must get all the answers to his questions from within himself. Neither Asita, nor any other priest, could guide him to the heart of darkness where, he imagined, lay the mystery of creation.

One night, he again decided to slip out of bed, while Yashodhara lay fast asleep. Just beside the bed, Rahul lay in his crib, wide awake. Although the room was quite dark, the flames in the fireplace gave out enough light to help Siddhartha look around.

He bent over the crib and picked up Rahul in his arms. The child began to look intently at his father. Two pairs of eyes were now in close communion with each other. He saw an enigmatic smile rippling across the child's face.

Gently, Siddhartha carried him in his arms to the window. Outside, the moonlight lay like a white sheet all over the ground. So bright was its silvery glow that the stars were almost indiscernible.

Looking into the deep pools of Rahul's eyes, he murmured, 'I love you.' Then, as if reflexively, the child's little fingers began to run all over his father's face.

Suddenly, Siddhartha heard the bed creak, and there was Yashodhara staring at both father and son.

'Are you sure you haven't disturbed him in his sleep?' she asked.

'No, he was wide awake when I picked him up . . . in fact, we were conversing when you intervened.'

Smiling, she said, 'Conversing with that mute little thing?'

'No, dear Yasho, silence speaks its own language . . . I tend to think that a little child's perception of the world is far profounder than an adult's, because his mind can penetrate the mystery that veils human existence. It is only when he begins to speak, argue and wrangle that he loses his supersensory perception of life.'

'I don't understand what you are saying,' she said.

'But Rahul understands my language, for isn't he my creation?'

'Ours!' she exclaimed, smiling.

'Indeed,' responded Siddhartha. 'I think he's already mature enough to understand many things.' He paused. 'Have you noticed that he never cries? A child cries only when something confounds it. But Rahul is already an adult . . .'

There was a brief spell of silence. Then Yashodhara spoke, somewhat sternly. 'But I don't like you carrying him to that window, lest he become a brooding dove, like you.'

'Who knows what he will become, Yasho?'

'There you go again, teasing me.'

She stepped forward to take Rahul into her arms, saying, 'It's my turn now.' But, surprisingly, the child resisted being taken away.

Rahul was then put into their bed, where he lay between his father and mother.

'That's better,' quipped Yashodhara, 'because now we can share him equally.'

'No, some day I'll let you have all of him, all the time.'

'Another riddle?' she asked.

6

For several weeks, Siddhartha was lost in meditation under his favourite tree. All sorts of questions kept bobbing up in his mind, like bubbles rising in a boiling pot. Then, one afternoon, after a long session of deep meditation, he rose, like a man just waking after a long dream. In his eyes was a strange sparkle as if he were communicating with some other world.

Later that evening, he went to Channa's cottage. A gentle knock at the door brought him out.

'Can I talk to you about something very urgent?' Siddhartha said. 'But not here. Let's go somewhere else.' Then, pointing to a rock, on the edge of a flower bed, he said, 'How about sitting there?'

'Anywhere,' replied Channa. 'But that otherworldly look in your eyes . . .' he broke off.

'I need your help,' Siddhartha said in a pleading tone. 'I can't turn to anybody else.'

Looking perplexed, Channa said, 'Please come out with whatever you have in mind. You know I'd do anything for you.'

'Anything?' Siddhartha asked.

'Absolutely. But, please, what's it that you want me to do?'

'I have decided to renounce everything . . . I must go away. There is no rest for me till I find an answer to the great riddle of life—the genesis of pain and suffering.' He paused. 'I know Asita will not be of any help to me . . . I never told you that I attended several sessions in the audience hall—cases of lust, greed and violence . . . what's the way out of this life's web?'

Channa kept looking at Siddhartha's face, with a long, cold stare. He was perplexed, not knowing what to say. Then he said, 'But your child, O Prince, and Yashodhara. What have they done to be suddenly forsaken? And would King Suddhodana be able to survive this shock?'

Heaving a deep sigh, Siddhartha replied, 'Time will sort it all out, somehow.' He took a long breath and resumed. 'Of course, the hardest wrench would be leaving behind my little son. You know, I had a little talk with him last night. I held him in my arms, and I thought we could communicate with each other. Since my blood flows in his veins, he'd certainly understand why I have taken this desperate decision.'

'But why can't you wait a year or two?'

'No, Channa, it would then become much harder. Rahul would pull me down like a millstone round my neck. So I have chosen what seems to me the right moment to go away, like a bird leaving its nest behind, its eggs still unhatched.'

Channa took a long time to reply, taking it all in.

'Where do I come into this scenario?' he asked.

'I'd like you to drive me out of the city. Of course, I'll be in my royal robes so that we could slip out, unsuspected.'

'When do you want to do it?'

'Tonight—at the stroke of midnight.'

'Oh God!' exclaimed Channa. 'I wish you'd talk to Kanaka as well.'

'He'd understand, like my Rahul. You know, horses have a supersensory perception, like babies.'

'I'd do it for you, dear Prince, but do you realize how I'll feel parting from you?'

'You'll have to do this for me,' said Siddhartha. 'This will be our first step towards detachment.'

It was then decided that he'd come to Channa's cottage precisely at midnight. Since it was a bright moonlit night, the operation had to be carried out very cautiously.

As Siddhartha arrived at the stroke of midnight, some clouds appeared in the sky, as if nature also wished to collude with him.

Finding himself yoked to the chariot at this odd hour, Kanaka looked curiously at his master.

'Since this will be our last ride together, dear Kanaka,' Siddhartha said, 'be prepared for the parting tonight.'

Kanaka snorted as if he'd sensed it all. He pricked up his ears, and began to rub his muzzle against his master's right shoulder. Siddhartha then got into the chariot, and beckoned Channa to ride away. A gentle caress of Channa's right hand, and the horse broke into a gallop. At the front gate of the palace, the gatekeeper stopped the chariot to see who was riding in it. Recognizing the chariot's occupants, he thought the prince was out for a ride in the moonlight. As the chariot sped by, Siddhartha looked back at Kapilavastu, the city of his childhood and youth.

They drove far out of town till they reached the bank of the river Satya, across which lay a dark forest. Here they saw a boatman sleeping in his boat. Awakening him, Channa asked if he'd ferry his master across the river. The man was groggy and reluctant. But as soon as Siddhartha presented him with a gold ring, the man untied the boat and readied himself for the ferry.

Siddhartha then asked Channa to wait till he changed into plain clothes—a saffron robe and a white dhoti. Now looking like a sadhu, he turned to Channa. 'Here are my royal robes and my jewellery. You may take all this to Yashodhara as I am now all set to travel light. Taking a diamond ring off his right hand, he said, 'This is for you, dear Channa.'

'No, Prince, it would appear as if I have been rewarded for this little service.'

'I know it, Channa,' Siddhartha said, 'Still let this ring stay with you as a memento from me. It's just a token of my deep affection for you . . .'

Channa broke down. Reclining his head against the flagstaff of the chariot, he started crying bitterly.

'Don't cry, Channa,' consoled Siddhartha. 'It was perhaps ordained that you'd usher me into the unknown.'

Then he turned to Kanaka who'd watched it all silently. When Siddhartha caressed his muzzle, and then let his fingers run over his flanks, the horse gave out a long, heart-rending snort which sounded like the anguished wail of a dying animal.

'You see, Prince, he too is heartbroken. I think this moment of parting has shattered him.'

'Man can never equal an animal's capacity for feeling,' Siddhartha said. 'If Kanaka could speak, he'd have surely asked me not to forsake him. Maybe, we'll meet again, though only after I have achieved my mission. How very paradoxical that while I'm venturing out to understand the genesis of pain, I have caused so much agony to you, Kanaka and my family. I already tend to think that nothing is attainable without sacrifice.' Then, looking wistfully at Channa, he added, 'Tomorrow is going to be an exacting day for you. I don't know how you'll be able to explain all this to my family. But you will do it, I'm sure.'

He then turned to the boatman, and said, 'Let's go, friend.'

Till the boat had gone deep into the river, Siddhartha saw Channa standing tearfully on the bank, with Kanaka snorting, fitfully.

Since the clouds had now melted away, the moon emerged in its full glory. On the placid surface of the river, its reflection looked like a human face, wan and despondent. In the still silence of the night, Siddhartha heard the splashing of the oars in the water. Rhythmically, they dipped and rose, like a pattern in some musical notation.

Seeing Siddhartha lost in thought, the boatman refrained from saying anything. He was the kind of man who never spoke while ferrying anyone across the river. It was only when he touched the other bank that he asked, 'Sir, where will you go from here?'

'I don't know.'

'But the forest is deep and dark,' he said.

'I know.'

Thanking the boatman for a smooth sail, he stepped out and started walking through the forest. Being barefoot, he knew he should walk carefully, skirting all briars and brambles. Since he was now wedging deeper and deeper into the forest, the moonlight vanished, and it became pitch dark all around.

He sat on a rock for a while to rest his weary limbs. As he looked about, he saw a fire a little distance away. Since it had become quite chilly, he decided to go towards the fire. But as he approached the spot, he was shocked to see that it was a cremation ground, and the flames were rising from a dead body just cremated.

A voice then rose from behind the pyre. It was a sadhu, barely clad. He was drinking water from a skull held in his right hand. Siddhartha was completely unhinged at this grotesque sight.

'Who are you, young man?' asked the sadhu. 'If you are feeling thirsty, you may drink from this skull, or I can get you another . . .'

Horrified, Siddhartha said, 'No, I am not thirsty.'

'I can see that you are scared to see me drinking from a skull. But, remember, that if you live in close proximity to death, day and night, you'll never lose your sanity. Death is the only vantage point from which you can see human life in a correct perspective. Those who remain oblivious of their end chase mere shadows—lust or greed.' He paused. 'You know, I sometimes imagine that the skull I am drinking from was once the head of some beautiful dancer, who danced with her hips swaying, her long dark tresses swinging around her shoulders, like incensed snakes.' Then, pointing to another skull lying close by, he added, 'And that one, presumably, was of some rich farmer, who owned several paddy fields, and pots of gold stacked away in a cellar of his house. But where has it all ended?' Then, looking closely at Siddhartha, he asked, 'Why are you wandering about in this dark forest?'

Already touched by his observations on death, Siddhartha told the sadhu why he'd renounced a princely life to understand the purpose of existence. 'I am very fortunate to have met you,' said Siddhartha. 'I'll always remember you as my first guru.'

'You seem to be a highly motivated young man,' said the sadhu. 'Surely, you'll achieve your mission. Why don't you stay here with me for a few days, and I'll share with you whatever I have learnt in life.'

'Indeed, O Master,' responded Siddhartha.

That night, he slept, for the first time, on bare ground, with a log of wood as his pillow. Next morning, the sadhu awoke him, gently touching his feet.

'Let me take you to a pool, just a mile away from here, and you'll meet a friend of mine there.' Then, smiling, he added, 'It's a lion. Since there is only one pool in the forest, all sorts of animals come there to drink. But you'll see that even wild animals are harmless—they will attack you only if you provoke them. It's only human beings who kill each other mindlessly.'

As they both walked over to the pool, each holding a skull, they heard some rustling in the bushes on the other side. Then a lion emerged in its full regal majesty, its eyes glowing with the pride of a monarch who rules over the forest. It threw an inquisitive glance at the sadhu, as if asking, 'How is it that you have brought a guest with you this morning?'

But as they both filled their skulls with water and rested for a while, the lion also drank some water, and then lay full-length on a patch of grass, basking in the warm early sunshine.

'Do you see how animals can instinctively feel the warmth of fellowship?'

During the next four days of his stay in the forest, he had to live ascetically, like the sadhu—on green leaves and fruits. This took a toll on Siddhartha's body, which became weaker and weaker till his ribs started showing through his robe. But what sustained him in the forest was his daily conversation with the sadhu, listening to his insightful observations on life.

'If the body is just a vesture for the soul,' the sadhu said one morning, 'why should a human being burden it with heavy clothes, even in winter? If naked we came into this world, and naked we'll depart, why should we dress up?'

Another day, he came up with an interesting thought. 'I'd say that even truth gets muzzled under a heavy layer of clothing. In any interaction between two souls, why should there be this iron curtain of dress? So I respect nudity as a worthy posture of the soul, because it recognizes openness in word, thought and deed.'

But soon Siddhartha realized that austerities could also enfeeble the soul. Doesn't one's thought process also get impaired by fasting over a long period of time? Slowly, Siddhartha began to comprehend the truth behind the adage that a sound mind resides only in a sound body. This realization dawned upon him when he felt distracted during his meditation.

It was now time to leave the forest. But he let the sadhu know how very enlightening his discourses had been. He sought his blessings and then parted from him.

7

A few hours' walk from the forest brought him to a small village, Udupi. It was in a state of excietment because of a wedding. In front of the wedding procession was a group of singers, dancers and drummers who were being cheered by all the onlookers. What a contrast, he said to himself, to the cremation ground where he had spent a few days with the sadhu. When the procession went past Siddhartha, who was walking along a pavement, he caught a glimpse of the bride peeping out of her palanquin. As he saw her bedecked with jewellery, he said to himself, 'There hangs a skull on a living body!' What was the difference between a funeral and a wedding procession? he wondered. Just the difference between a palanquin and a bamboo pyre?

Since he'd fasted for a few days, he felt quite hungry. Round the street corner was an eating place, crowded with customers who were gorging themselves on meat, rice and liquor. When Siddhartha put out his right hand to a young man for a handful of rice, he was brushed away.

'There goes someone who begs for food without doing any work,' the young man taunted. 'A parasite, isn't he?'

Hurt, Siddhartha was about to walk away when an old man took pity on him, and offered him some leftovers on a plantain leaf. With gratitude, Siddhartha accepted the food. As something in his voice touched the old man, he asked, 'What's your name, young man?'

'I don't have any name, sir,' he replied. 'I'm just a wandering mendicant . . .'

What's there in a name? Siddhartha said to himself. Did that sadhu in the forest have any name? Do skulls carry any names?

The old man's question set off a host of thoughts in his mind. Wasn't the assertion of identity linked to one's ego, which always raised barriers between human beings? Wasn't there also a state of mind when one just felt like a straw blown about by an idle wind? If only one could empty out one's mind of all worldly thoughts, close one's ears and eyes to all sounds and sights . . . but was such a state possible?

As he was engrossed in these musings, he heard some shouting a little distance away. It was a market square where a small crowd of street urchins had hemmed in a young bull. As they shot arrows from their bows at the helpless animal, it bellowed out in deep pain, gushing blood everywhere. Its flanks riddled with arrows, it tried to break through the ring, but there was no exit, so it squirmed and wailed. Each time it tried to gather itself up on its tottering hooves, it slumped onto the ground.

What cruelty, Siddhartha said to himself. Threading his way through the crowd, he called out, 'Isn't this an inhuman sport, young friends? Why are you out to kill a helpless animal that has not done you any harm?'

A voice rose from the crowd, 'Get out of our way, you beggar! You are a spoilsport . . . we are only playing a manly game.'

Having failed to dissuade these blood-thirsty killers, he walked inside the ring, and stood close to the bull. Then, raising both his hands, he said, 'Is this sport manly or unmanly? Would anyone of you have dared to face this bull single-handed in a forest?'

But when his pleading also failed, Siddhartha said, 'All right, why don't you get me first? Maybe, it would be a more exciting sport for you to shoot down a human being.'

As a hush fell over the place, and all shooting ceased, Siddhartha bent over the bull and started pulling out the arrows, one by one. Then he tore a piece of cloth from his robe and began to wipe the blood from the animal's body. As the bull now struggled to hold itself up on its legs, Siddhartha caressed its head, its neck and flanks. A look of gratitude now appeared in the bull's eyes. Wagging its tail, it began to lick his hands. Then leading the bull to a gap in the encircling crowd, Siddhartha let it hobble away.

Turning to the urchins, he said, 'Do you know what that bull whispered into my ears when I was wiping off its blood? It said, "Forgive them all as they knew not what they were doing."'

Hanging their heads in shame, the urchins melted away. Siddhartha then recalled how Devadatta, his cousin, had wounded a swan with his bow, while he had picked it up to fondle and caress it.

Siddhartha was again lost in thought. Why was man a complex creature, a queer blend of compassion and cruelty, of love and hate? He came to the conclusion that in the hierarchy of all creatures, animals scored over humans.

Later in the evening, he sat under a tree and went deep into meditation. For several hours, he was lost in the deep recesses of his mind. When he opened his eyes, he was surprised to see at his feet, a plantain leaf loaded with rice and fruits—and near it was a brass bowl full of milk. Who was this unknown person who had made such a thoughtful gesture? he wondered. He decided to carry the bowl with him everywhere, and to accept, unreservedly, whatever was dropped into it.

Next evening, when it was time to eat, he stopped in front of a house, holding the bowl in his right hand. As he knocked at the door, a beautiful young woman came out.

'A handful of rice, O lady, if you please,' Siddhartha said.

But the woman just stood there, staring at his face. Then her lips curled into a seductive smile and she said, 'Indeed, not just a bowl of rice, but a night's rest as well.' She paused. 'Since you look tired, wouldn't you like to rest your weary limbs in my bed? My husband is gone to another village for some work, and I am feeling cold and lonesome. And you are so handsome!'

Siddhartha at once understood her intention. Wasn't she another woman like the farmer's wife, driven by lust?

Turning to walk away, Siddhartha responded, 'No, thanks. I am neither tired, nor too hungry.'

So disgusted was he with the woman that he decided to skip his evening meal.

Since his stay in Udupi had not been too happy, it was time, he thought, to leave this village early next morning.

8

It took him a couple of days to reach Magadha, which had the same regal atmosphere as Kapilavastu—caparisoned chariots, riders on horseback, elephants lumbering down the streets, crowded marketplaces and spacious parks. He walked into the central park, chose a quiet spot under a large banyan tree, and went into meditation. Fascinated by this handsome, young yogi with long hair falling over his shoulders, a small crowd of men and women gathered around him. When he opened his eyes, he saw at his feet a large plantain leaf, with fruit, rice and vegetables laid out on it. He acknowledged the crowd's hospitality with folded hands.

A woman, with a small boy, stepped forward and placed him at his feet, saying, 'O Swamiji, will you bless him? He has been sick for a couple of days, and I'm worried.'

Smiling, Siddhartha said, 'But, Sister, I am not a vaidya who can cure any ailment.'

But when the woman persisted in asking for his blessing, he caressed the boy's head. Now happy, the woman walked away. The next day, she returned with her son, and said, 'My gratitude to you, O Swamiji, because your blessing has worked. My son is now up and about, fully recovered.'

Siddhartha couldn't explain to her that he had not worked any miracle, and her son's quick recovery was just a coincidence.

In Magadha, Siddhartha didn't have to go from door to door for food, as it was brought to him every day.

One morning, he was confronted with an embarrassing situation. As he opened his eyes after a long spell of meditation, he saw an old woman, with tears streaming down her cheeks.

'O Lord, I entreat you to save my only son,' she implored. 'He is dying, and all vaidyas have given up on him. Now you are my only hope. Please . . . !'

Siddhartha tried hard to explain to her that he didn't have any miraculous power. Falling at his feet, and crying bitterly, she still continued, 'But you cured an ailing child only the other day.' She paused. 'That woman is my neighbour, and word has gone around that you can work any miracle.'

He pondered over the situation for a while, quite perplexed. Then he spoke gently and compassionately.

'Dear Mother, if your son is terminally sick, what comfort can I give you? Death is something nobody can vanquish.'

But the woman didn't give up, and kept looking at him with intense yearning and hope in her eyes.

'I know, Swamiji, that you can salvage my son from death. I beg of you . . .'

He then thought of a way to wriggle out of the situation.

'All right, I'll try to help your son,' he said. 'But there's a condition.'

'Any condition . . . my son is the sole reason for me to live. If I lose him, I'll immolate myself.'

'I do understand your pain,' he said. 'But as I've already said, there's a condition attached to my offer.' He paused. 'Will you go to any house and bring me a handful of mustard seeds? But, remember, that it must be from a house that has never seen death. If you succeed in finding a family in which nobody has ever died, come back to me and I'll cure your son.'

Excited, the woman hurried away.

At the first door she knocked on, she was received very graciously. When she asked for a handful of mustard seeds, the housewife rushed inside and brought her a bagful of mustard seeds.

'Why just a handful, Sister, when I can gladly spare a bagful? I hope this will do.'

Delighted, the woman accepted the gift. But then she asked if there had been any death in her family and promptly came the answer, 'I lost my father only last month, and I'm still grieving . . .'

'I am saddened to hear this,' the woman said. 'In that case, I must return your mustard seeds as they won't help me. Let me thank you nonetheless.'

She received the same response as she went from door to door. So death was omnipresent, a raven that flapped its ominous wings over every family.

When she returned to Siddhartha, and reported it all to him, he flashed a smile. 'So you see, Mother, nobody can escape Yama—man, animal or bird. That which is born must die.' He paused. 'Even the avatars and rishis had to die—Krishna, Rama, Vishwamitra. So why be fearful of death? Let it happen any time. The only way to conquer death is to engage oneself in righteous action. One can then breathe one's last composedly, fearlessly and stoically . . . Death is just shedding one's body and liberating the soul from the prison of the mortal frame. It is like moving from one house to another. Like taking off one's night clothes to put on a new dress the next morning.'

Then he told her how he'd spent a few days with a sadhu who lived on a cremation ground and drank water from a skull. That sadhu believed that living in close proximity to death enabled one to face it courageously.

Although Siddhartha's words awakened her to a new realization, she still could not overcome her pain. Distraught and saddened, she trudged away.

As everyone in Magadha now heard about a handsome yogi who discoursed on life and death, crowds began to swell around him. People came to listen to him, taking the banyan tree's canopy as a temple's dome under which this enlightened sage gave his discourses.

Then, one morning, he saw the crowd giving way to a royal charioteer. On hearing about the yogi, King Bimbisara and his wife had decided to seek his blessings. Maybe, the yogi could bless them with an heir to the throne. As the chariot stopped, Siddhartha saw the royal couple alighting from it. The king then walked up to him, bowed and said, 'My town is blessed with your presence, O Swamiji, I've heard about your miraculous powers. Maybe you could bless us too.'

At this point, the queen joined in. 'We are unfortunate to have remained issueless. My husband has performed all kinds of rituals but . . .' she trailed off.

Understanding their predicament, Siddhartha said, 'Birth and death are beyond human control. Just as death comes to us unexpectedly, so does birth . . . I don't know how Magadha has come to believe that I can work miracles. I am just a wandering mendicant.'

Smiling, the king responded, 'All sorts of sadhus and swamis have visited the city, but never anyone as enlightened as yourself.'

A long spell of silence fell between Siddhartha and the royal couple. Then the king spoke in a voice, intense and plaintive.

'I have no right to ask you about your family, although I feel instinctively that you are of some noble lineage . . .' He paused, fumbling for words. Then he brought himself to speak out: 'Although we have no issue, we still have the choice of adoption. So . . . if only I could adopt you as my son and install you as the crown prince of Magadha, I'd thank the gods for this boon. I'd then meet my death with a smile on my face.'

Siddhartha was deeply touched by the king's words. He remained speechless for a while. Then he broke into words. 'If only I could tell you what I've already renounced in life . . . but all that must remain sealed in my heart. I'd just say that I've set out on a spiritual voyage, and I won't let any temptation come in my way. I propose to stay in your city for a couple of days more, and then resume my journey.'

Speechless, both the king and his wife, kept staring at Siddhartha's face.

'Then I should not be an impediment in your way,' said the king. 'I'll indeed pray for the success of your mission . . . but may I still ask a favour of you?'

'Anything I can do, within my powers.'

'Would you promise to visit Magadha again after you've achieved your mission?'

'Absolutely.'

'Then there'd be something to look forward to,' said the king. But as his charioteer cracked his whip in the air to prod the horses into motion, Siddhartha leapt to his feet.

Drawing close to the vehicle, he said to the driver, 'I implore you, O friend, not to use your whip on these helpless horses. Aren't they handsome creatures; their flanks glittering in the sunshine, their manes glossy as any yogi's long hair? Wouldn't it hurt you if someone were to give you a lash on your back?'

Listening to Siddhartha's gentle admonition, the king turned to his charioteer. 'No more whipping hereafter, Sanya. Let's understand what the yogi has just said.'

'But, Swamiji,' said the charioteer, 'I do feed them very well . . .'

'Food is not the only thing a creature needs, man or animal. It is also love and compassion.'

As the chariot rolled away, the crowd reassembled. An old man then spoke out. 'Today, I saw the supremacy of spirituality over earthly power.'

9

It was about noon when Siddhartha reached Greha, a small town on the northern border of Magadha. As he entered, he felt something ominous about the place. A sandstorm suddenly erupted and swept across the streets and bylanes.

With the exception of a few grocery shops, all the other shops sold only meat or liquor. On the pavements, he saw men, half-drunk, staggering on their feet, quarrelling with each other over trivialities.

Siddhartha stopped in front of a shop that sold pet birds and animals—parrots, sparrows, puppies and cats. He was saddened to see these helpless creatures in cages, denied the freedom of open air. When the shopkeeper asked him if he'd like to buy any bird or animal, Siddhartha replied, 'I don't have the money to buy off your entire shop, to set prisoners at liberty.' He paused. 'How would you feel if you were locked up in a solitary cell?'

'Get lost!' the man shouted at Siddhartha. 'If you are acting like a god, your place is in a temple, not here.'

Deeply hurt, Siddhartha walked away.

When he knocked at the door of a house for food, he was given half-cooked rice and stale milk. At a street corner, he was stopped by a man holding a bottle of liquor in his right hand.

'Let me pour some of this stuff into your bowl, O Swami,' he said. 'It's *soma ras*, divine nectar, which will take you to *svarga*.'

'No, thanks,' said Siddhartha. Then, with a sneer on his lips, he added, 'Is it nectar or drain water? That bottle will carry you to *naraka*.'

'Get away,' the man yelled at Siddhartha. 'I'd have hit you with this bottle, but I'll let you go this time.'

A strange town, Siddhartha said to himself. He learnt, for the first time, that humiliation could also lead one to self-realization. Didn't it need some spiritual strength to absorb insult and injury?

He wasn't surprised to learn that whereas Greha had a number of brothels, there was only one place of worship, the Shiva temple. Siddhartha was now determined to explore this strange town.

As he was walking down a bylane, he saw three men standing in front of a single-storey house. Intrigued by their conversation, he stood behind them, eavesdropping.

'Won't you let me go in first,' said a balding, short-statured man to the other two, 'since I was the first to arrive here?'

'There is no queue system here,' quipped the tall, lanky man with a scar on his left cheek. 'She will take me in the moment she sees me. Because I give her a silver ring for two hours in bed, and a gold ring for the entire night. Expensive she is, but she gives me my money's worth.'

'It's not the money alone that works with her,' intervened the third man, who was younger than the other two, and was handsome and virile. 'She wants both cash and fun in bed. And let me tell you, I can perform better than anybody else in town.'

Siddhartha was disgusted to hear this lewd conversation, which revealed to him the seamy side of human nature.

The three men suddenly became conscious of another presence behind them.

'Look,' said the balding man, turning around, 'there is another customer too—young, virile and handsome. He may knock us all out.'

'Indeed,' said the young man. 'You know, these sadhus can work miracles in bed.'

'And they carry enough money too,' joined in the tall man. 'They beg during the day, and collect enough cash to squander it away on a whore.'

Siddhartha heard it all. He now understood that these men were there to spend the night with some prostitute, who lived in the house across the lane. He decided to watch the scene.

There now appeared at the doorstep a beautiful young woman, draped in a translucent saree that exposed all the contours of her body her breasts, thighs, and legs. A pair of diamond earrings dangled from her ears and around her neck was a pearl necklace. Her complexion was white as jasmine, and her eyes sparkled. A perfect temptress, Siddhartha said to himself. Why had she chosen this ignoble profession? he wondered. Astonishingly beautiful that she was, she could have easily found a husband, raised a family with children, and lived a life of peace and happiness. But she'd obviously fallen for greed—gold, diamonds and pearls.

Siddhartha was taken aback when this woman walked straight up to him, rudely ignoring the other three men. When those customers noticed that the sadhu had scored over them, they trudged away, visibly humiliated.

The prostitute's eyes were now riveted on Siddhartha's face, and from her mouth drooled the saliva of lust. In a voice, husky and seductive, she said, 'You are so young and handsome. Why did they keep you waiting so long?' Then, tantalizingly, she added, 'They come here like honey bees, calling me their "nectar" and "rose". But I can fathom it all . . .' Then, drawing close to him, and holding him by the hand, she cooed, 'Come in, my swami, right into my bed and into me. It doesn't matter if you can't pay me. Let it be a deal in kind, not cash.'

Flinching, Siddhartha said, 'O lady, you have mistaken me for a customer. I just happened to stop by . . . as for me, I am on a voyage into the unknown. Sort of an exploration . . .'

'What could be more exciting than exploring a woman in bed?' She smiled. 'Come voyaging into my bed . . . . I've never met anyone like you. Of course, I've had priests too. For instance that Brahmin from the Shiva temple. He comes to me twice a month, late at night, after ringing the bells and chanting mantras—his face covered with a shawl. But he comes only for a fling, you know what I mean. I pity him, because he's only a voyeur—stays in bed the entire night, touching my body all over, my breasts and thighs. But he is incapable of doing anything. Oh, that impotent wretch! But he brings me a ruby ring each night, sometimes even a diamond bracelet. All stolen, I guess, from Lord Shiva's idol—offerings to the god from his devotees.'

Siddhartha flashed a broad smile. He now understood that even the so-called holy men visited prostitutes.

'I don't know why I have shared all this with you,' she resumed, 'at our very first meeting. Maybe because I have fallen in love with you, something I've never done so far. Is it Kama Deva's floral arrow that has transfixed me? So come in, my love. Why are you holding me out here in suspense?'

'No, I'd like to talk to you out here,' Siddhartha said.

'So strange,' she said, her forehead wrinkled. 'My name is Dharmi, and what's yours?'

'I have no name, presently,' he responded. 'I'll let you have it when I acquire one.'

'So tantalizing you are—and that's what makes you all the more adorable. Can't you hear my heart throbbing, and hot blood racing through my veins?'

'Not quite,' he smiled. 'But I can see it all on your face.'

'Oh, you are teasing me,' she said. 'So near and yet so far away.'

Siddhartha now brought himself to asking her what she thought of her customers.

Her eyes flashing with disdain, she said, 'Street dogs they are, all of them. I offer each of them my body, like a bone thrown to a dog. Well, I have to earn my livelihood, somehow. Where is a place to live honourably in this god-forsaken town? This is the place for pimps, bootleggers, rapists and thieves.'

'It's a sordid world, indeed, inhabited by godless people,' Siddhartha sighed. 'But wouldn't it be a challenge to show them some light?'

'But they are mice—they'd scamper away if you showed them any light. They prefer to revel in darkness . . . I told you about that priest who visits me, his face covered so that even his Lord Shiva may not recognize him.' Then, looking directly at Siddhartha, she added, 'But I haven't told you that I never offer anyone my self. I always hold it back as something more precious to me than all the rubies and diamonds I get . . .'

'O Gracious! O Heaven!' Siddhartha exclaimed. 'This is detachment of the rarest kind and I'd, hereafter, look upon you as one of my mentors. Let me touch your feet . . .' But as he gestured to kneel down, she drew back.

'No, I'd much rather you touched my lips,' she said. 'I wish you'd kiss me, just once,' she implored. 'Sleeping with you would be like making love to a god who could claim both my body and soul.'

Empathizing with her emotion, he said, 'I am not a god and making love is not the only way to happiness.'

'There you go again, teasing me,' she said.

As they were talking, the evening began to deepen into darkness, but the wind was still blowing. Suddenly, it swelled into a storm, which began to rattle the doors and windows of Dharmi's house.

'You may at least come inside to carry on this conversation,' she said.

'No, we can talk out here . . . darkness and stormy weather don't bother me.'

'But what if some other customer showed up here . . .'

'Never mind, Dharmi. This is an open talk between two friends . . . I wouldn't mind if somebody else also joined in.'

She gave in to him, having failed on all counts.

'All right,' she said. 'But where will you sleep tonight? In some ashram or temple?'

'No,' came the prompt answer. 'I always prefer to sleep under a tree, or on a pavement—anywhere in the open. Sleeping on the ground makes me feel close to earth.'

Smiling, she said, 'Suppose, I too come along with you to sleep under a tree, or on a pavement, near your feet . . .'

'It would be very uncomfortable for you . . . it takes a long time to get used to sleeping on bare ground . . . most men live in fantasy, sleeping on thistledown beds, with a new woman each night.'

'How true!' she concurred. 'I feel as if you are leading me into another world, quite alien to me. Yes, I'd like to be seduced by you, because seduction has been my way of life. But this time, I'd like to be seduced out of my sinful life . . . would you tempt me, O stranger?'

Deeply touched, Siddhartha said, 'You don't have to be tempted by anyone, because you are already a blessed creature.'

'That's plain flattery,' she said.

'No, it's the stark truth.' Siddhartha countered. 'By now, you must have realized that I'm not the kind who'd indulge in deviousness or prevarication. Truth is what I'm seeking in life.'

'I can see that,' she said. 'But since you have raised a storm in my mind, I dread the thought of losing you.'

'One can also live in remembrance,' he said. 'For instance, I'll always remember you as someone who taught me detachment and transparency of thought and feeling.'

She then spoke like someone possessed, 'Listen, I have just decided to give up my profession and live a solitary life. I propose to keep my front door always locked to keep those "dogs" away, and come in and go out of my house from the rear. This will give everyone the impression that I have fled the town . . . all this because I'll always cherish the memory of knowing you, as my only love.'

Overwhelmed by her vow to give up her profession, he said, 'You are the stuff gods are made of. You have learnt that without renunciation, nobody can attain divine bliss . . .'

A brief silence fell between the two.

'May I ask a favour of you?' she said, her eyes focused on his face. 'I wish I, too, had a bowl for you to drop something into.'

'Anything that I can really do,' he answered.

'Would you visit me, just once again? Because the very thought of your return would sustain me.'

Promptly, Siddhartha replied, 'Certainly, dear Dharmi. In fact, next time I may even spend an entire night with you, not just an evening.'

'Is it true?' she asked, her eyes sparkling.

'Absolutely.'

'Then there'll always be a candle illuminating my dark nights,' she sighed. 'Fare thee well, O stranger. Now go forward to achieve whatever goal you've set for yourself.'

'Take care, Dharmi.'

'You too.'

Siddhartha walked away with a host of thoughts and feelings surging in his mind. As he looked back from the street corner, he saw her wiping her tears with the hem of her saree. Pain—isn't it a double-edged weapon that both singes and soothes? How would she have felt if he'd told her that he was a married man, with a son? Then he asked himself—wasn't her renunciation as agonizing as his?

He decided to leave Greha the very next morning, bittersweet as his experience of the town had been. But before leaving, he decided to see the priest at the Shiva temple. Wouldn't it be interesting to meet someone who personified the utter perversity of the human mind? His sinful conduct was all the more deplorable since he was untrue both to himself and to his Lord.

Siddhartha arrived at the temple that same evening. He saw the priest sermonizing to a few devotees who were listening to him in rapt attention. Quietly, he sat in the last row, behind a pillar, unnoticed by anyone.

'What redeems man ultimately is the purity of his mind and body,' the priest was saying. 'But that is possible only through rigorous self-scrutiny. You may slip into the mire of lust if your faith in the Lord fumbles and falters.

'Man's greatest frailty is his vulnerability to carnal desire. Why did God create woman? I often wonder. The answer is to test our will to live piously. He who can overcome his carnal desire is blessed by the gods. Let us look upon every woman as our mother, sister and daughter.'

Sermon over, all the devotees bowed to the priest before leaving. Stung by this man's hypocrisy, Siddhartha walked up to him and said, 'What you just said is indeed the essence of our scriptures. But isn't there a vast hiatus between precept and practice?'

Looking at Siddhartha, a sadhu in saffron, the priest felt a little self-conscious.

'Were you in the temple when I talked to the devotees?' he asked.

'Yes, I was sitting behind a pillar. I agree that one should look upon every woman as one's sister, mother and daughter.' Then, probing his face, he asked, 'Can't a woman be a prostitute as well?'

The priest blinked and went mute for a while. 'Yes,' he mumbled as the word 'prostitute' almost got stuck in his throat. Staring at him, Siddhartha said, 'Because a woman as a prostitute may interest you, particularly.'

This innuendo stung the priest. But, thank God, the priest said to himself, how would this wandering sadhu know anything about his visits to Dharmi? Still, feeling rattled, he said, 'I'm afraid I have to do my puja in the sanctum sanctorum. So, please . . .'

That was a signal for Siddhartha to leave. But he was certain that the priest would now do some soul searching. In any case, the next time the priest chose to visit Dharmi's house, he'd find the front door locked.

10

As he walked out of Greha, and took the road to nowhere, his mind kept returning to Dharmi who'd shown him a new facet of detachment. In what way was her renunciation less painful than his? If he had renounced his family, and the pomp of royalty, she too, had given up her profession which provided her an affluent lifestyle. A feeling of guilt gripped his mind—wasn't he responsible for pushing her into deprivation? There was, however, one difference between her sacrifice and his. While he'd gone into exile for self-realization, she'd chosen to live as a recluse in her own house, out of unrequited love. Immersed in these thoughts, he walked on till afternoon deepened into evening.

Suddenly, he saw a man walking up to him from the opposite direction. Greeting him with folded hands, the man asked, 'O Swamiji, have you come to Uruvala for the first time?'

Siddhartha understood that the man had taken him for a sadhu, dressed in saffron, holding a brass bowl in his right hand.

'Yes,' said Siddhartha.

'I am a farmer, returning home after the day's grind,' the man said. 'Since you look tired and hungry, why don't you rest for the night in my cottage and have a meal with my family? My cottage will be blessed with your presence.'

'Thank you very much, dear friend. How very gracious of you to offer me your hospitality,' said Siddhartha.

It was a thatched cottage, just a room and a courtyard. The farmer laid out a mat on the floor of the room, and gestured to Siddhartha to sit on it. The farmer's wife and their 5-year-old son came out. As soon as Siddhartha looked at the boy, he recalled Rahul, whom he'd last seen in the crib. He must have by now grown into a boy, like this farmer's son. As moisture welled up in his eyes, he jerked his head to shake himself out of this memory. No, he shouldn't lapse into attachment—that way lay pain.

'Tell Swamiji your name,' the farmer said to his son.

'That's not necessary,' said Siddhartha. 'We can be friends without knowing each other's names.'

He then asked the boy to sit beside him on the mat while the farmer's wife prepared the meal.

Siddhartha began to teach the boy the gayatri mantra, highlighting its emphasis on equipoise in life.

'In this boy's case, Swamiji,' intervened the farmer, 'it is all play and no work.'

'At his age, play's the thing,' said Siddhartha. 'There'd be enough time, later in life, for him to work for his livelihood.'

Meal over, Siddhartha lay on the mat and slept for the night. Since the farmer was up at dawn, ready to leave for work, Siddhartha also picked up his bowl to depart. But before leaving, he thanked the farmer and his wife, and blessed their child.

As he stepped out, the early sun shone brightly on the streets of Uruvala. The farmer's warm welcome had already set the tone for his stay in this town. Walking through the streets, he stopped by a pond, shaded by trees. As he sat on a rock, gazing at the pond, two swans waddled up to him and began to quack, as if they were greeting a new visitor to town. The birds even let Siddhartha caress their soft, white bodies.

Then he rose to explore the town that had already fascinated him. As he walked along the pavements, he noticed that most of the shops sold flowers and incense. Was it because Uruvala had a large number of temples, always crowded with devotees who came with flowers as offerings to their deities?

What a contrast to Greha, thought Siddhartha. It was indeed a blessed town, a place to converse with priests and sadhus. When he asked someone about the most popular place of worship, he learnt that it was not a temple but an ashram run by a sage, Apara Kalama, who gave discourses every evening.

The same evening Siddhartha was at the ashram, known as Shanti Nivas, where a large crowd had gathered to listen to the sage. At sunset, the sage appeared in the front yard of his ashram, sat on a platform, acknowledged the crowd's greetings, and began to speak.

'One of the greatest weaknesses in us humans is the assertion of our identity, our ego—"*Aham*, I am!" Not only does it alienate us from each other, but it also blinkers our vision of truth, which reveals its true face only to a man who can see beyond the narrow confines of his self. Self-assertion raises its ugly head right from our childhood, from the day a child is named. As it grows, it begins to brandish its caste and status. This is because we forget that since birth is only an accident, we just as easily could have been a Brahmin or a Shudra. Then why glorify one's name and position which are only accidents of birth?

'Take a bird—a sparrow, parrot or nightingale. Once it is caged, it is named. There it now stays behind bars till it ends up as a handful of feathers to be thrown away on a pile of garbage. So it is with any animal that is adopted as a pet. Therefore, non-identity is a state of the mind known only to free birds and animals. Any human being conditioned by identity is susceptible to pain and suffering. Why should a man court sorrow when he is created to be free and happy?'

A hush fell over the crowd as everyone was swept away by the sage's words.

Then came the time for questions. It was Siddhartha who rose to ask, 'O Sage, although I am still under the spell of your discourse, I am nagged by a question. If man is destined to be free and happy, why has God created evil? If He is all-merciful, why has He bound us to sorrow? Why is someone born blind, deaf or dumb? Also, is non-identity enough to salvage us from pain?'

All eyes turned to this sadhu in saffron, so young and handsome.

'Creation of evil is God's way of testing our judgement to choose,' replied the sage, 'between right and wrong. We are granted the freedom to opt for salvation or damnation. God's remote eye only scrutinizes whether we opt for truth or falsehood. If we can control our ego, our obsession with identity, we can soar high like an eagle, unfettered.'

Though still perplexed about God's intention, or even His existence, Siddhartha chose to remain silent.

As the discourse ended and the crowd dispersed, Kalama himself walked up to Siddhartha and said, 'Looks like you've just arrived in town.'

'Yes, Guruji,' responded Siddhartha.

'If you have no place to stay, you may live at my ashram,' said the sage. 'I am impressed by your zeal to know and think independently. You seem to be a highly motivated seeker.'

'I'd consider myself very fortunate to be your disciple,' said Siddhartha. 'I can't thank you enough for giving me the privilege to stay at your ashram.'

'But,' said Kalama, 'you'll have to observe the rigorous routine of the ashram—rising before dawn, meditation for an hour and then doing such chores as cooking in the community kitchen, sweeping the floors . . .'

Bowing his head, Siddhartha said, 'I'll gladly submit myself to the ashram's discipline.' But, he added, 'May I, please, have some private sessions with you, whenever you can spare the time?'

For a moment, the sage seemed to be pondering over something. Then he responded in a voice, soft and gentle. 'In your case, I'll make an exception. You may join me during my morning walk, after meditation . . . So we'll be able to walk and talk . . .'

'I am greatly honoured,' said Siddhartha.

Next morning, after meditation, Siddhartha waited eagerly for the sage to appear in the frontyard of the ashram. When he started walking alongside the sage, he was excited. Their first stop was the same pond where Siddhartha had rested for a while. Here, Kalama stopped, took out some particles of rice from his pocket, and threw them to the same pair of swans. The birds came out of the water and wadded up to him, as if to greet a friend. He then went down on his knees, and began to fondle the birds.

'They are my friends,' he said, turning to Siddhartha, 'and we meet every morning before I leave for my long walk.'

Siddhartha then told him how he, too, had befriended these birds, the first day he entered Uruvala.

'You may consider yourself very fortunate,' said Kalama, 'because these birds don't come near anyone who looks unfriendly.'

As they walked out of town, they climbed up a hillock that overlooked the town and sat on a rock. Looking directly at Siddhartha, Kalama said, 'Look out there, at the sun's visage . . . I think it looks like God's face, resplendent in its divine glory.'

There was a brief silence between the two. Then, hesitatingly, Siddhartha said, 'In your discourse, last evening, you referred to God's remote eye . . . but I tend to think that instead of invoking God in every situation, we might just concentrate on righteous action . . . as for God, He may be just a figment of our imagination.'

'I admire your boldness, young man,' said Kalama. 'But I have no right to force you into my way of thinking. You may choose your own path, from darkness to light.'

The sage was now convinced that his disciple was a true seeker.

On their way back, they stopped by the pond again. But this time, the sage walked over to the rear side and looked at a tortoise, which had withdrawn its limbs into its shell.

'Here's another friend,' he said to Siddhartha. 'But this morning, it appears to have gone deep into meditation, its eyes and ears closed to the world outside.'

11

That evening, Kalama's discourse was both entertaining and enlightening. He started in a light vein:

'This evening, I'd have brought my guru here to let him enlighten you on how to lead a spiritual life. But he would have found it difficult to climb up onto this platform. Also, he speaks only through his eyes and gestures.' He paused. 'Well, my guru is a tortoise.'

A mild ripple of laughter ran through the audience. Everyone looked forward to what the sage would say next.

'It was Rishi Panini who was the first to allude to a tortoise, in the *Yoga Sutra*, as a creature capable of controlling its limbs. He, therefore, used it as a symbol for his yogic asana—to enable human beings to achieve longevity, peace and health. Later, Lord Krishna exhorted man, in the Bhagavadgita, to imbibe the example of the wise tortoise which can, whenever necessary, withdraw its organs under its shell to manifest the mind's supremacy over the body.

'One of the wisest creatures on earth is, therefore, the tortoise but, like any other bird or animal, it remains nameless. I wonder if you know that a tortoise's span of life is very long—it can live for hundreds of years. What then is the secret of its longevity?

'First, it takes life calmly, without any stress, which is the bane of human existence. Aren't most of us prey to anxiety, always worried about what the future may hold for us? We are always caught in a rat race, jostling over each other, to press ahead for some material gain. On the other hand, a tortoise is free of this tension. Leisurely, it crawls from one place to another.

'This is manifested in its respiratory system. It takes six or seven breaths in a minute while a human being, always stressed, takes about seventy breaths a minute. This may unravel the mystery behind a tortoise's longevity. The slower the pace of life, the longer its span. So let us not race for material advancement, but work just as much as is necessary to keep our body and soul together. Contentment and patience are the bedrock of a happy and long life.

'Also, while human beings expend too much energy in meaningless verbal wrangling, a tortoise just perceives and understands. In fact, we can learn from birds and animals the value of silence. No wonder, sages observe *mona vrata* for the greater part of each day, for this is a very effective way to conserve our physical and mental energy. Why speak when silence and gestures can express thoughts better?

'But what makes a tortoise a spiritual creature is its power to subjugate its organs, which are the portals of desire and anxiety. Desire manifests itself in many ways but, primarily, as our carnal yearning. So while we let our desires carry us away, like an unbridled horse, a tortoise can keep its organs muzzled. It has the will to withdraw them under its impregnable shell. While many a sage, in his unguarded moment, has been seduced by lust, a tortoise can never be caught napping.'

As Kalama concluded his discourse, a pall of silence descended upon his listeners. When he asked for questions, there was no hand raised, because the entire crowd was still under his spell. Smiling, he pointed his finger at Siddhartha, but even he had no question to ask this time.

When Siddhartha accompanied Kalama the next morning, he couldn't help complimenting him on his discourse.

'How very privileged I am,' he said, 'to have you as my spiritual guide.' Then, smiling, he added, 'Don't you think that we should install in every temple the idol of a tortoise?'

Kalama smiled. 'But did you notice,' asked the sage, 'that while I emphasized the spiritual nature of a tortoise, I also had in mind the namelessness of all birds and animals?'

'Indeed.'

'As my favourite disciple, I now wish to ask you,' said the

sage, 'to expand your compass of non-identity, to include non-being as well, for that is what elevates a man to a much higher plane. Non-being is a much loftier state of mind that even non-identity.'

Siddhartha looked puzzled, for he'd just heard something that he didn't quite comprehend.

'This non-being is called *akinconnayatana,*' resumed the sage.

Looking a little perplexed, Siddhartha said, 'I'm afraid it's the usage of Sanskrit that often obfuscates a simple concept.'

'I agree,' Kalama said, 'but this new concept is for only you, since you are an extraordinary seeker. Now let me explain to you what is meant by non-being.'

They were now both sitting on top of the hillock overlooking the entire city of Uruvala.

'Non-being,' Kalama explained, 'simply means total cessation of all physical and mental activity, a sort of annihilation of both mind and body. It may seem something impossible to achieve, but it can be attained. The first step towards this mental state may be taken through a yogic exercise—*shavasana.* Let me demonstrate to you how to do it. Never mind the Sanskrit terminology, for I agree that it's the doing that really matters.'

Then he asked Siddhartha to lie on the ground, his arms stretched along the body's left and right sides. The next step was to imagine life draining out of the body, limb by limb—first the head, then chest, thighs and, finally, the toes. 'One should now imagine,' he said, 'that one's body is a corpse, all sensation gone. It is, in fact, like sleeping in death. This is the way to experience non-being, which not only gives respite to one's body and mind but also re-energizes them.'

'If you can do it a couple of times every day, you'll feel rejuvenated,' said Kalama.

So excited was Siddhartha that he did this yogic exercise a dozen times the next day. But whereas he was able to let his body go limp, the sensation of non-being still remained elusive. So, the next morning, when they were together on top of the hill, he put it straight to his guru.

'I did it several times yesterday, O Master, but I couldn't get the experience of non-being.' Then, looking directly at him, he asked. 'May I ask you something?'

'Go ahead.'

'Have you ever experienced this sensation of non-being, yourself?'

There was a long silence. It seemed as if the sage was lost in introspection. Then, taking a deep breath, he replied. 'Never.' He paused. 'A couple of times, I deluded myself into thinking that I'd got there . . .' He trailed off. 'But I feel that since I'm now at the dead end of my own spirituality, I cannot guide you any further. As you are an irrepressible seeker, you'd have to either get it all out of your own self, or find some other guru.' Then he added, 'Why don't you consider going to Gaya? There's a yogi there, Swami Nityanand, who runs an ashram near the confluence of the rivers Mohini, Niranjana and Falga . . . of course, you'll carry my blessings with you wherever you go.'

It was with a very heavy heart that Siddhartha bade farewell to Kalama. But before leaving the next morning, he lay prostrate at his feet. Then, rising, he said. 'O Master, I'll always remember you for your guidance but, above all, for your integrity and transparency.'

12

It was a long, exhausting walk of three days and nights, without any food or water. When he stopped at any wayside village, and put out his bowl to any house-holder for food, he was turned away. He felt as if he'd walked out of *svarga* to get lost in *naraka*. Depression, exhaustion and deprivation now began to weigh him down.

At the end of the third day, when hunger began to gnaw into his vitals, he recalled the hungry man he'd encountered in the marketplace with Channa—his hollow, sunken cheeks and the look of acute pain in his eyes. It was now Siddhartha's turn to experience that sensation of hunger. His stomach was like a river slowly drying up to leave only lines and curves on its sandy bed. Still more agonizing was thirst. If hunger had weakened him, it was the tongue that was now parched, withered like an autumn leaf.

Exhausted, he lay under a tree to rest for the night, but

sleep eluded him. Sleep is for those, he realized, who have a hearty meal, and a comfortable bed to lie on.

Late after midnight, he somehow managed to doze off. But when he opened his eyes at sunrise, he was horrified to see, behind his head, a huge king cobra poised on its coiled tail. Its hood looked like the coronet of a monarch, and its eyes glowed like burning coals.

In spite of the danger looming in front of him, Siddhartha watched the creature closely—the pattern on its hood, its intricate design in multiple colours.

Surprisingly, the cobra did not move at all. Why had it come there, and how long had it stood in that posture? Siddhartha wondered. Then, it dawned upon him that the cobra had stayed there all night to protect him. This became evident when the snake folded its hood, and gently slithered away behind a bush.

Siddhartha resumed his journey, still agonized by hunger and thirst. By the time he reached the outskirts of Gaya, he was reduced to a skeleton. But he walked on till he reached the confluence of the rivers Mohini, Niranjana and Falga.

For a while he sat on the bank of the Mohini, wondering whether he should drink its water, which looked somewhat muddy. But, stung by thirst, he decided to risk it. Just as he picked up a palmful of water, someone from behind touched his right shoulder and said, 'No, this water is not potable.'

As he turned around, he saw a woman standing behind him, holding something in her hands.

'Here is some rice pudding for you, and a glass of milk,' she said.

Siddhartha was speechless. He was so overwhelmed that he couldn't utter a word; he just kept staring at this woman.

'My name is Sujata,' she said. Then, pointing her finger at a cottage closeby, she added, 'I live out there.'

'I don't know how to thank you.' Siddhartha said. 'I haven't eaten for four days . . .' He then helped himself to the pudding, and drank the milk. Revived, he said, 'Maybe you could also help me to locate the ashram run by Swami Nityanand.'

'But he passed away just three days ago,' she said. 'He'd been ailing for quite some time. A great soul he was . . . The entire town came to his cremation, with wreaths of flowers.'

'I came here all the way from Uruvala to become his disciple,' Siddhartha said, sadly.

'I was also at the cremation, selling flowers,' she said. 'My husband is a florist, he runs a shop downtown.' Then she added compassionately, 'Why don't you rest for the night at our cottage?'

'Thank you very much, Sister, but I'm used to sleeping in the open, under a tree, or on a pavement, to feel the warmth of the earth under me. Also, it's now late spring, and sleeping on the bank of this river would be refreshing.' Saying this, he turned to walk away towards the river.

Lying on its bank, he gazed at the moon sailing across the sky, in all its majesty. Its reflection shimmered in the limpid water. It seemed as if there were two moons communicating with each other. But since the moon in the river was closer to him, he began to look at it very intently. Suddenly, he became conscious of a human face in the reflection—a pair of eyes under a broad forehead. Then a voice rose above the lisping waters.

'It was ordained that you'd be denied the guidance of Sage Nityanand,' said the voice. 'Now that you are on your own, you'll have to get all the answers from within yourself. So look not for any sage in Gaya, for there's also a sage within the deep recesses of your own soul. Let him lead you to your destination.'

As a cloud covered the moon, its reflection, and the voice, vanished.

He now realized that if he was destined to see the divine light, it would be in Gaya and nowhere else, because place and time are coordinates that forge their own configuration to shape human destiny. In his case the place was to be Gaya, and the time late spring.

So he decided to choose an appropriate spot in Gaya where he could go deep into meditation, and not emerge from it till he'd seen the light beyond darkness. His wheel had come full circle since his wedding night when the razzle-dazzle outside the window had beckoned him to look into the heart of darkness.

After a restful sleep that night, he awoke refreshed. All day he kept walking down the streets and bylanes of Gaya, looking for a quiet spot for his meditation. Late in the evening, as he turned into a marketplace, he caught sight of a mammoth peepal tree, which fascinated him immensely. It looked like a temple, with its top like a dome, and its stout trunk like a pillar supporting the entire structure. As he stood gazing at the tree, with its sprawling branches, he imagined it to be a multi-armed deity, beckoning him to come to it. At the bottom of the tree was a platform of granite stone on which, he felt, he could sit and meditate. He recalled what the voice had told him that, finally, he would have to get all the answers from within himself, especially when destiny had denied him the guidance of Swami Nityanand. So he decided to sit cross-legged under this tree, and meditate.

Since it was now late evening, he saw the moon rising on the horizon, like a silver bowl. As its light filtered through the leaves and branches of the tree, it cast shadows on the ground, which looked like a jigsaw. In this mental state, he imagined the jigsaw to be a riddle that he was destined to solve.

He closed his eyes and felt like a diver who'd plunged into a deep river, and was now penetrating its depths, layer by layer, from non-identity to non-being. Or was he like a fish sailing in and out of the rocks and ferns of a coral sea? How very cool and tranquil it was in this subliminal region, away from the din and turbulence of the world above, where human beings groaned and wailed in pain and suffering!

As he imagined that he was about to touch the bottom of the river, he heard a voice which distracted him. He opened his eyes and saw an ebony-faced man standing in front of him.

'I've been shadowing you ever since you left Kapilavastu. I saw you cross the river Satya and walk into the dark forest where you spent a few days with that sadhu—and then I watched you all through your wanderings. So, you see, I've been a sort of fellow-traveller to you, sharing all your thoughts and feelings. When you had that brief encounter with Dharmi, I thought for a moment that you might go to bed with her. But you seem to be made of much harder stuff than even a tortoise's shell.'

Although Siddhartha was intrigued to learn that this man knew all about him, he said, 'You seem to have a glib tongue, and if I've let you blabber on, it is out of my compassion for you, because you sound like a troubled soul. Shame on you, however, for your lewd remark about me and Dharmi . . . in any case, who are you?'

'Nameless I must remain, for namelessness is what you also consider synonymous with non-identity. But let me assure you that I am your well-wisher. A true friend, you know, is one who helps by speaking out the truth, howsoever bitter. So may I, please, shake you out of your complacency?'

'All right,' Siddhartha responded, out of desperation to get the man off his back as soon as possible. Siddhartha's voice was stern and wrathful.

'There, you have lapsed into anger, a frailty you must overcome if you wish to achieve your goal.'

The man had indeed scored a point over him by provoking him into anger.

'Well, I'm all ears, but don't hold me very long, please,' said Siddhartha.

'Thank you very much,' the man said, smiling.

'First, let me ask you if you were justified in forsaking your wife and son. What sin had they committed to be abandoned so callously, while you set out to seek self-glorification as a spiritual leader? I tend to think that you exult over being revered as a swami. How did you feel when King Bimbisara knelt at your feet to seek your blessings?'

Hurt by his barb, Siddhartha reacted sharply.

'First, let me say that when I left Kapilavastu, it was not desertion of my family. I'm sure that my family has understood what I am trying to achieve. Don't forget that sacrifice is the only way to salvation. Because the way to take is to give.' He paused. 'And as regards my brief encounter with King Bimbisara, it was with great humility that I received his greetings.'

'That's an inane rejoinder, lacking any conviction,'

countered the man. 'You seem to be adept at verbal jugglery . . . in any case, the worst thing you did was to torture your body by subjecting it to mindless austerities. The body is a gift from God, to be nurtured on food and drink. Why were we humans endowed with a mortal frame when we could have been created as just souls, flitting about in the air, denied the pleasure of touch and smell?'

'The body was not created to indulge in sensual pleasures,' countered Siddhartha. 'It was created only as an instrument of prayer and meditation, not as a vessel of filth—desire and lust.'

His eyes flashing, the man retorted, raising the pitch of his voice. 'Then why did God create man and woman? Was it to see their hands raised only in prayer, and not to fondle the contours of each other's body? I'm sure you understand what I mean.'

'I can see that you are trying to uphold sex as the only legitimate human activity,' said Siddhartha. 'But if man could sublimate this energy, he would attain spiritual bliss. That's how Lord Shiva acquired his shakti.'

'But he also slept with Parvati,' the man jibed. 'Worship of the linga is also a way to attain spiritual bliss.'

'The linga is a symbol of procreation, not indiscriminate sexuality,' retorted Siddhartha.

The man responded, with a wry smile on his face. 'An interesting notion—this concept of procreation. I ask you to answer me truthfully—when husband and wife make love, do they think solely of procreation? Doesn't lust enter into the act of love?'

'No, making love can also be just a conjugal duty.'

'How did you conduct yourself in bed on your wedding night, O Siddhartha?' asked the man, grinning.

'I just did my duty as a husband,' he replied. 'The very next morning, I went to Channa, my charioteer, to share with him my dilemma. I even asked him if I should have married at all.'

The man blinked his eyes, perplexed.

'Look,' said the man, 'if your body can relish Sujata's rice pudding after a period of hunger, it can also savour a little sex, which can replenish one's energy.' Then, after a pause, he added, winking, 'Menaka didn't bring Sage Vishwamitra a bowl of rice pudding and a glass of hot milk. Instead, she tempted him into drinking from her breasts the nectar brewed only for the gods in *indraloka*.' Another pause. 'Well, I too, have a surprise for you. I have brought my daughters here, each more beautiful than the other, to let you have the pick of them. This is the time and place, O man, to abandon yourself for a while—springtime, moonlight and sex under the protective cover of this peepal tree. It's now or never. Let not this moment slip away . . .'

A feeling of utter revulsion rose in Siddhartha's mind. What kind of father was this man, to offer his daughters to him for the night? Not even a procurer would stoop so low.

'Although you seem to be some evil spirit from *naraka*,'

said Siddhartha, 'I have no hatred for you, only compassion. I know it's your function to waylay innocent people. Still, I hope that you have some modicum of decency left to admit that you have miserably failed to seduce me. May I request you to leave me alone?'

Suddenly, the man bowed to kiss Siddhartha's feet. Then, looking up, he said in a voice, now soft and tender. 'I am Mara, the tempter, and I give in to you, O Prince Siddhartha. Yes, I did try all my wiles on you, but they were to no avail. All my arrows fell blunted against your body, as impregnable as a tortoise's shell. Surely, you are destined to see the Divine Light tonight, and right here under this tree . . .' Then, looking beseechingly at Siddhartha, he implored, 'I entreat you to pray for my soul as well.'

A smile flashed across Siddhartha's face as he raised his right hand in a gesture of blessing.

It was the third quarter of the night, about an hour and a half before dawn. The entire town of Gaya lay deep in sleep. There was no movement of any kind on the streets. Since the moon was now hidden behind a cluster of clouds, darkness had fallen all over the town.

Still sitting cross-legged under the peepal tree, Siddhartha again went into meditation. Deeper and deeper he sank into the layers of his mind. Then, suddenly, a light entered his brain. It was so bright that he felt he could see through even the pitch darkness. A strange sensation of a new awakening rose within him. He felt like a dead man rising from his pyre. He then heard a voice in the air, soft and gentle:

'You have arrived, O Siddhartha. Unnecessarily, you wandered from one place to another, interacting with sages, when the answer to the great riddle of life lay right within your own self. Not through listening to religious discourses, not through ascetic austerities, or study of the scriptures, can one attain divine bliss. The path to salvation is simple and direct—through righteous action. It's a path with eight landmarks—right perception, right thought, right speech, right action, right pattern of life, right mindfulness, right endeavour and right concentration. Now you may go into the world and share this with all human beings.

'As for yourself, you'll no longer be enmeshed in the cycle of birth and death, because you are now blessed with nirvana. So death will seize you only once—and then no more. Also, hereafter, you will be known as the Buddha, the enlightened, and not Siddhartha.'

Siddhartha, now the Buddha, rose to his feet, like a man in a trance. Before he could say anything to the voice, it had vanished into the darkness. An awesome silence now descended all over the place.

Suddenly, the moon broke loose from the clouds. As its beams filtered through the leaves and boughs of the peepal tree, the moonlight cast shadows on the ground. However, this time he didn't see a jigsaw, but a distinct pattern with a centre and eight concentric circles around it.

Where should he go from here? he asked himself. If some benign destiny had taken charge of him, then let it also guide his steps. Maybe he should go to Kashi, he thought, the holy city of the Ganga. It took him a couple of days to get there. But when he found the banks of the river crowded with all sorts of sadhus who chanted mantras mindlessly, he decided to move on to some other place, smaller and quieter. When he reached Sarnath, he stopped. Here was a small town that seemed to be an ideal place to deliver his first sermon.

13

After walking about the streets and bylanes of Sarnath, the Buddha came to a park. He chose a tree near a fountain, sat cross-legged under it, and began to meditate. When he opened his eyes, he saw some people standing around him. Smiling, he greeted them with folded hands.

It was a mixed crowd, though most of the people seemed to be daily wage-earners. An old man came forward and said, 'O Sage, we have been waiting for you to come out of your meditation. We can see from your resplendent face that you understand the secret of life. So we are eager to hear you.'

Briefly, the Buddha told the gathering how he had travelled far and wide in search of peace, and how it was in Gaya where, one night, he saw the Divine Light. He spoke in Pali, and in a voice that sounded like the chiming of bells in a temple.

'We all know,' the Buddha said, 'that we are caught in a web of suffering. We groan as we grind through our daily routine. We come into the world crying, and we leave it with tears in our eyes. It is this pain that prompted me to find some way to conquer it. *Dukha* is our lot. But there is a way out of it.' He paused. 'Not through austerities, nor through study of the scriptures can man attain peace. In vain do our priests lead us through a labyrinth of obscure religious concepts when the answer to the riddle of life is quite simple—righteous action and detachment. While our mentors never forget barriers between man and man, between a Brahmin and a Shudra, I believe that, since birth is only an accident, any man, be he a sweeper or a cobbler, can rise to the highest level of divine bliss—if he performs his duties righteously, regardless of any reward. So even a Shudra can attain the status of a Brahmin, if he engages himself in disinterested karma.' He paused. 'So I invite you all, dear friends, to enter a temple that is open to everyone, a temple without any deity or sanctum sanctorum, a temple whose doors are open day and night. In fact, this temple is within ourselves because, deep down in our minds, we all know what is right or wrong. We know that it is desire that leads us astray—our pursuit of money or fame. And that way lies suffering, because material gain is ephemeral. What does sensual pleasure bring us? A momentary joy, followed by sorrow. A farmer who ploughs his field dutifully is far happier than a rich merchant who sleeps restlessly at night, dreaming of wealth. Little does he realize that contentment is far more rewarding than greed.'

As the Buddha stopped, a hush fell all over the place. Such was the magic of his discourse that many listeners felt as though they had been transported into a new world.

Then rose a man, dressed in soiled clothes, holding a broomstick in his right hand.

'I am a sweeper, O Sage, shunned by everyone as an untouchable. I am not allowed to enter any temple, or even stand near an eating place. Even my shadow is considered ominous. But I have a beautiful daughter who was molested by a Brahmin, two days ago. Where shall I go to seek justice?'

The Buddha held the sweeper's hands compassionately and said, 'These temples are places where greed and hypocrisy reign. So why should you even care to enter such places of worship?' He paused. 'And as regards your daughter, the divine hand of justice will take care of that Brahmin.What a hypocrite that man was who believed in untouchability and yet tarnished his own body and soul by outraging the modesty of an innocent, helpless girl!'

All those who heard him console the sweeper were deeply touched by his words. When the crowd melted away, a young man stayed back. Dusky complexioned, he was tall and lean, with a strange sparkle in his eyes. On his left cheek was a mole, and his forehead was wrinkled. Drawing close to the Buddha, and bowing reverentially, he spoke in a voice that sounded like a broken reed.

'My name is Ananda, O Swamiji,' he started. 'I'll need some time to come to, as I'm still under the spell of your words.' He heaved a deep sigh, cleared a lump in his throat before he resumed. 'I've known pain in all its diverse forms—disease, domestic violence and what not. I've seen my father beat my mother every day. My elder sister is estranged from her husband, and my maternal uncle is bedridden with some indeterminate ailment. Coward that I am, I decided to run away from home. I have wandered all over the country, visited such sacred places as Prayag, Haridwar, Kanyakumari and the Shiva Linga temple atop a hill in Srinagar. But whenever I sought solace from priests, they doled out only words, words, words. Yes, I've heard all those high-sounding mantras. And then came your soulful discourse this morning. Still, may I ask you, O Sage—is pain really conquerable? Is there any panacea for sorrow?'

'Absolutely.' There was a definitive ring of assurance in the Buddha's simple reply.

The Buddha then asked Ananda to sit beside him, and said, 'You seem to be a soul in distress. But what has touched a deep chord within me is that you have wandered around, like me. I see in you a kindred soul.'

There was a brief pause after which Ananda asked in a pleading voice, 'Would you, O Swamiji, take me as your disciple? Because I feel that you alone can guide me out of the deep and dark tunnel of my suffering.'

'Indeed, you'll be my first disciple, the first monk in the sangha that I propose to set up here.'

'I am blessed,' Ananda responded, joyfully.

'As regards your question whether suffering is conquerable or not,' said the Buddha, 'I'll answer it tomorrow evening when I deliver my first sermon.'

'I'll be there, O my guru,' Ananda said, like a child who'd been promised a toy.

'I've chosen Hanuman Square as the venue of my sermon. I'd be happy to see you there, Ananda.'

Since word had already gone around that an enlightened sage would address the residents of Sarnath, a large crowd showed up. The Buddha was happy to see Ananda sitting in the front row.

It was an early winter evening, with a mild nip in the air. Since morning, it had been drizzling, with dark clouds sailing across the sky. At noon, there was a downpour which made the streets wet and slippery. But, surprisingly, the weather became clear in the afternoon; the sky was now bare, and the atmosphere cool and bracing. Ananda, who'd feared that the inhospitable weather might keep the people away, was happy to see a large gathering present to listen to the Buddha.

After briefly describing his encounter with the Divine Spirit under the Bodhi tree, the Buddha began his discourse.

'We all know that sorrow stalks us throughout our life in the form of deprivation, sickness or death. So the prime problem for man is to liberate himself from pain. If we are born into suffering, and we die in pain, is there relief from pain? The answer is yes, indeed. Let me now share with you Four Noble Truths.

'The first Noble Truth, as I have already said, is suffering.

'The second Noble Truth is that all pain has an origin which can be identified.

'The third Noble Truth is that pain can be conquered.

'The fourth Noble Truth offers us liberation from suffering, if we follow the eight-fold path that I will now explain. This path is like a wheel with eight spokes, each holding the wheel together, and not letting it fall apart.

'The first spoke is right perception, which is the capability to see human experience in a correct perspective. We suffer when we take a warped view of life, coloured as we are by our personal prejudices.

'The second spoke in this wheel is right intention. If our motivation is correct, we cannot go wrong. The fruit of any action which is born of bad intentions will inevitably be bitter.

'The third spoke is right speech. A man who speaks truthfully without prevarication or dissimulation, is already on his way to peace. A spoken word can both hurt or heal. So let us choose our words carefully, because an unkind word can cause a wound that no balm can heal.

'The fourth spoke in this wheel is right action. Let us engage ourselves in righteous acts which are not tainted by any ignoble intention—greed, jealousy or pride. An action done dutifully, regardless of reward, is a sure pathway to bliss.

'The fifth spoke is right livelihood, because much depends upon the vocation we choose. How can one attain peace if one is engaged in such a profession as burglary, usury, gambling . . . ? So let us choose our mode of livelihood thoughtfully, with great care and discretion.

'The sixth spoke is right endeavour. If our effort is geared to some unrighteous act, we are doomed to unhappiness.

'The seventh spoke is right mindfulness. Since our mind is an unbridled horse, it must be reined in at every step. Let us always be mindful of which way we are going. Since our mind is a wayward monkey that leaps from one treetop to another, it must be muzzled. Right mindfulness alone can help us attain equipoise and tranquillity.

'Finally, there is the eighth spoke—right concentration. It is, of course, an aspect of right mindfulness. If we concentrate our minds on the right things, we will never feel miserable. Meditation, which is based on right concentration, is a panacea for all mental ailments. It helps one dissolve one's tensions. A stressed-out person courts pain, while a person concentrating tranquilly on noble thoughts savours peace and happiness.

'So here is a pathway to peace, open to everyone, regardless of caste, colour, creed or status. In vain do we wander from place to place, seeking enlightenment from seers and sages—the cure for sorrow lies in this eight-fold path. Yes, any man can achieve nirvana, liberate himself from the cycle of birth and death, if he follows the eight-fold path that I have just expounded. Then one can say to death—haven't I conquered you? Let me now recite some verses that express a man's experiences when he attains nirvana:

Many a mansion have I lived in,
seeking him who fabricated this prison
of senses, steeped in sorrow.
Such was my endless struggle.

But, O architect of the mud-house,
now that I have seen thee,
never again shall I let you build these walls
of suffering, nor nurture this lofty tree
of falsehood, nor raise new columns
of clay. Demolished is this house
its columns fractured—
all designed by deception! Now I shall
voyage forward to my ultimate goal
—Nirvana!

For quite some time everyone remained spell-bound. His words kept reverberating in the atmosphere. Then everyone rushed forward to touch his feet. It was as if a new star had appeared in the firmament, beckoning all human beings to shed their sorrows.

When the crowd dispersed, Ananda walked up to the Buddha and lay prostrate at his feet. Then, rising, he said, 'It was an awakening for me, O Lord. Now I know how to vanquish pain, and attain salvation.'

The Buddha asked Ananda to help him set up a sangha in Sarnath. As soon as a community of monks was established, he let Ananda take charge of it, while he himself set out to deliver sermons in the neighbouring towns and villages. For each of his public discourses he chose a single aspect of his eight-fold path.

It was after his sermon on righteous action in Santala, a small town near Kashi, that the Buddha met Sariputta, a stocky, short-statured man in his early thirties. He had the same eagerness of quest that the Buddha had seen on Ananda's face. Enlightened by the Buddha's exposition of disinterested action, he also sought to be taken as one of his disciples. He was then directed to contact Ananda in Sarnath and join the sangha. Similarly, he took another disciple, Moggallana, into his fold after his sermon on mindfulness in Gorinath, a village near Gaya. Meanwhile, Ananda was also giving discourses on his master's concept of dharma. So remarkable was his memory that he could not only reproduce his master's teaching, word by word, but also speak in a similar voice, gentle and persuasive.

In a short while, the sangha in Sarnath grew into a large fraternity of monks and nuns. Every devotee was required to observe a rigid routine of meditation, frugal diet and simple dress. With their cropped heads, saffron robes and bare feet, these monks and nuns looked like divine spirits in mortal frame.

To the Buddha's dismay, dissensions and jealousies began to surface in the community. However, with gentle persuasion, Ananda was able to keep the flock together.

The real opposition to Buddhist dharma came from the followers of Lord Mahavira, who'd died a few years earlier. The Jains tried hard to wean away as many Buddhist monks as possible, saying that their dharma was fake—too radical and simplistic. Above all, since it was silent about the existence of God, wasn't it like a body without a soul?

But, in spite of some dissensions simmering in the sangha, and the opposition from Jainism and orthodox Brahminism, the Buddhist dharma continued to appeal to the common man. The real forté of the Buddha's teaching was its use of simple Pali, its stress on social equality and its stress on righteous conduct.

Whenever the Buddha returned to Sarnath after his discourses elsewhere, he mingled with his followers as a simple monk—humble, gracious and unpretentious. Unless a teacher himself embodied his teaching, he would not be able to carry conviction in his words.

One day, as he'd just concluded his discourse on

forgiveness, he was taken aback to see Devadatta walking up to him.

'I know I must have surprised you. But here I am, standing in front of you, to plead guilty for all my wrongdoings. I also wish to hold onto your dharma of forgiveness and compassion. Would you, therefore, pardon me?'

'I forgive you and embrace you both as my cousin and friend.'

Looking immensely pleased, Devadatta said, 'Then won't you accept me as one of your disciples?'

'It would give me great pleasure to take you into my fraternity.'

But it didn't take Ananda too long to discover that his master had inducted into the sangha a wolf in sheep's clothing.

Devadatta's real motive was not only to incite trouble in the fraternity, but also build himself as a potential successor to the Buddha. To achieve his nefarious design, he even plotted to eliminate the Buddha. One evening, as the Buddha was in meditation at the foot of a hill, he asked one of his accomplices to hurl a huge boulder downhill. But, fortunately, the boulder rolled off a few yards away.

14

Utterly frustrated by the happenings in Sarnath, one morning the Buddha announced to Ananda that he would like to seek release, howsoever briefly, by undertaking a journey back to Kapilavastu. His first stop was Uruvala, where he'd spent some time under the tutelage of Kalama. Here he was given a very warm welcome by everyone at Shanti Nivas. Particularly excited was Kalama himself because his former pupil had now become the Buddha, the enlightened spiritual leader.

But when Kalama gestured to bow to him, the Buddha said, 'No, please, don't embarrass me as I'd still like to be considered your pupil. Don't forget that it was from you that I learnt to look within myself for the answer to the mystery of human existence and, above all, transparency and integrity.'

Touched by his words, Kalama said, 'It's your modesty

and humility . . . but now our roles are reversed. Hereafter, I'd look upon you as my guru.'

'Please don't say that ever,' said the Buddha.

When Kalama offered to reserve a special room for him at the ashram, the Buddha shook his head.

'No, Master, I'd prefer to stay with your other disciples, and follow the ashram's routine.'

Eagerly, Kalama looked forward to hearing how his former pupil attained enlightenment under the Bodhi tree. Next morning, when Kalama took him out for his morning walk, the Buddha told him how he saw the Divine Light and how Mara tried to waylay him.

'But what I learnt that night,' said the Buddha, 'may sound strikingly simple—that the way to salvation was just righteous action, that what obfuscates the common man is the theological casuistry of the priests.'

Kalama listened to him in rapt attention.

By now they'd climbed up to the hilltop where they used to engage themselves in long conversations.

'I have often wondered,' Kalama said, 'how the world came into existence. Did it surface from some vast ocean whose waters were calm and transparent? And weren't our first ancestors simple and tranquil creatures?'

'Even though you are fantasizing,' interjected the Buddha, 'I can see what you are trying to say—that our pristine way of life has now got vitiated by lust, greed and jealousy.'

'Then, isn't it our duty to somehow recapture that lost innocence?'

Nodding his head, the Buddha said, 'That's possible, but only through right thought and right action . . . that's what the Divine Spirit taught me.'

It was now time to climb down the hillock, and stop briefly by the pond. But the Buddha was surprised to see only one swan running up to him.

'What happened to its partner?' the Buddha asked.

'Died a few months ago.'

'How sad,' sighed the Buddha. 'This swan must be feeling very lonesome now.'

'No,' said Kalama. 'These birds don't grieve like humans. They face death stoically.'

'Indeed,' said the Buddha. Then he asked, 'Where is your guru, the tortoise?'

But when they turned to the rear, they found that it had gone under its shell.

'Gone deep into meditation,' said Kalama. 'Or maybe, it's observing *mona vrata*, complete silence, today.'

On their way back to the ashram, Kalama asked the Buddha if he'd consider giving a sermon that evening.

'No sermonizing here,' he said, 'because this is the place where I'd still like to learn much from you.'

'My only contribution was to send you to Gaya,' said Kalama, 'where the miracle happened.'

Next morning, when Kalama walked with him up to the

city's front gate to bid him farewell, he said, 'You did me a great honour by visiting me here. I will never forget that the Buddha stayed with me, even though it was for a day.'

15

When word reached Magadha that the young mendicant who had visited it some years ago, was now on his way back to the city as the enlightened Buddha, King Bimbisara was so excited that he ordered to have the city spruced up. A royal proclamation required all residents to put up floral banners of welcome on their housetops. The northern gate of entry was colourfully decorated as if a bridegroom were to be received by the bride's family. Men, women and children stood everywhere on the streets to greet the Buddha.

Since he was expected to arrive late in the evening, King Bimbisara ordered all citizens to welcome him with brass lamps in their hands. It appeared as if the city was celebrating a festival of lights.

But a wave of disappointment swept across the city when someone announced that the Buddha had already entered from the southern gate. This was followed by another disappointment because the city was suddenly caught in a storm. As it swept across the streets and bylanes, it blew off all the brass lamps. Darkness now spread everywhere, turning Magadha into a ghost town.

In the pitch darkness, the Buddha walked down a lonely street. As he approached a thatched house, he saw a poor old woman, holding an earthen lamp in her left hand. It was still burning, with her right hand protecting its puny flame. As for the wick in her earthen lamp, she'd torn a piece off her saree. There she stood patiently at her doorstep, waiting for the divine visitor.

A figure then emerged from the darkness, and stopped near the front door of her house. From the glow on his face, the woman instantly recognized the stranger as the Buddha. Holding the lamp in her left hand, she knelt to touch his feet.

'Is it a dream I am seeing, O Lord?' she stuttered, with tears in her eyes. 'Here you are, standing in front of my hut, now blessed with your presence.'

Raising her to her feet, the Buddha responded, 'It's a miracle of faith, O Mother. While the entire city is plunged in darkness, the only light visible is the feeble flame from your earthen lamp.' He paused. 'I don't know who is blessing whom . . .'

She stood speechless for a while, and then spoke in a voice choked with emotion. 'The king was expecting you to enter the city from the northern gate, and here you are at my doorstep.'

'I know it all,' the Buddha said, smiling. 'I do respect your king, and I'm looking forward to meeting him . . . But I deliberately chose to enter from the southern gate, because I wanted to avoid the fanfare.' Then, he added, 'The storm was not my doing . . . however, I am happy to see that while all other brass lamps have been blown off, your earthen lamp of faith has withstood the raging storm.'

Word then reached the king that the Buddha had already entered Magadha from the southern gate. There was a stampede of people surging southward, followed by the royal chariot in which rode King Bimbisara and his queen. As the chariot pulled up in front of the poor woman's hut, the royal couple got down. Then both the king and his wife knelt to touch the Buddha's feet.

'We missed you at the northern gate, O Lord,' said the king, with a ring of disappointment in his voice.

'But I'd have then missed this devotee, who holds the only unextinguished lamp, by the gate,' said the Buddha, pointing to the old woman, who stood embarrassed in the presence of the royal couple.

Then, turning to the king, the Buddha said, 'Haven't I kept my word? If I was eager to visit Magadha, it was only to meet you, because you are also upheld by faith.'

Touched by the compliment, the king said, 'I may be the king of Magadha, but you are now the King of kings. I can foresee that your message of love and peace will sweep across the entire Bharatvarsha.' He then implored the Buddha, 'Would you be gracious enough to stay at my palace as my honoured guest?'

'If I am not misunderstood,' responded the Buddha, 'I'd prefer to stay at this woman's thatched hut. But since your invitation comes not from the king of Magadha, but from someone whose faith is genuine, I cannot turn it down . . . but there is a condition . . .'

'Any condition, my Lord.'

'I will sleep on the bare floor, as I have always done,' said the Buddha.

'As you wish,' responded the king. 'I only want my palace to be blessed with your presence. In the annals of my kingdom, your stay here will be recorded in golden letters.'

The Buddha smiled graciously and got into the chariot, waving to the woman who still clung to her earthen lamp, which she decided to keep as a memento.

Next morning, there was a surprise awaiting the Buddha. As the king's attendant brought in two sets of breakfast—two bowls of rice and two glasses of milk—the Buddha asked, 'Why two sets?'

'The king also wishes to join you over breakfast,' the attendant replied.

A few minutes later, King Bimbisara walked in. Smiling, he sat beside his guest on the floor. 'May I, please, also have the honour of joining you over breakfast?'

Overwhelmed by this gesture of humility, the Buddha

said, 'You are a king who knows how to touch the hearts of others.'

King Bimbisara blushed, visibly embarrassed. Meal over, the king requested him to address his people that evening, if possible.

'I'd be delighted to speak to them.'

It seemed as if the entire town had turned out to listen to the Buddha. Although he repeated what he'd said in his first sermon in Sarnath, he now chose to dwell on the three concepts central to his teaching—restraint, compassion and peace.

Opening his sermon, he said that it is always the lack of self-control that drives man to misery. Indulgence in any form disturbs the equipoise of the soul. The golden mean is, therefore, the only path to happiness.

'Self-control is what man can learn from a tortoise, who knows how to withdraw its limbs under its shell, whenever necessary.

'Compassion is another virtue that we should cultivate—compassion for fellow human beings, birds and animals. It is the only way to soothe anyone in pain. If a man lacks it, he is like a rock, insensitive to feeling.

'But, above all,' he concluded, 'let us pray for peace for all living creatures. Shantih is an all-inclusive concept. Because unless we rid ourselves of such emotions as greed, jealousy and hatred, we cannot have any peace. Let us, therefore, pray for it—on the earth, in the air, and in the heart of every human being. If we want peace for ourselves, let us wish it for others as well.'

As he ended his sermon, he was cheered by his listeners.

When the king requested him to stay on in Magadha for a few days, the Buddha quipped that he was like a river that must flow on.

16

As he set out on his long journey to Greha, the Buddha felt that the tropical sun in its relentless fury made walking unbearable. Hardly had he walked a mile when he felt the need to rest in the shade of a wayside tree. He decided to walk only in the evenings, and then sleep under a tree at night.

As he reached the outskirts of Greha, he saw many people fleeing, carrying their meagre belongings on their heads. When he asked a middle-aged man the reason for this exodus, he was shocked to learn that the village had been stricken by plague and most of its residents had already migrated to other places. What would have happened to Dharmi? he wondered. If she had no place to go, she must still be in her house, locked indoors. The very thought of a destitute woman suffering from a deadly disease agonized him. But he was determined to honour his word.

As he walked through a marketplace in Greha, he stopped at a vaidya's shop. When he asked the man if there was any medication for the disease, the vaidya just shook his head.

'I have, however, an ointment which may give some temporary relief,' said the vaidya. 'But if anyone tries to apply it to a plague-stricken person, he'd also catch the disease, because it is very infectious.'

'Never mind that,' replied the Buddha. 'May I have some ointment, please? But I have no money . . .'

'Never mind,' the man repeated the Buddha's words. 'This is the least I can do for a sadhu.'

Thanking him profusely, the Buddha started walking through the streets, which were mostly deserted. He saw people wailing and groaning, with nobody to take care of them. As he turned a corner, he saw an old woman putting out her hand to him.

'Some water, please,' she cried out. 'I'm dying of thirst.'

Fortunately, he saw a pool close by. He filled up his bowl with water, and returned to the woman.

'Here is some water for you, Mother,' he said.

After drinking the water, she said, 'You seem to be a stranger here. This place is a *naraka*. You must run away as soon as possible.'

'No, I need to meet someone, whatever the risk,' he said.

Filling the bowl again with water, he walked on till he

reached Dharmi's house. He found the front door locked. Then he recalled that she'd decided to use only her rear door. Finding even that door locked, he thought she must have also fled the town.

But as he turned to leave, he saw a woman writhing in pain, just a few yards away from the house. When he drew close to her, he was stunned. There lay Dharmi, her hair like bristles, and her face festering with boils.

'Dharmi!' he exclaimed. 'Look, I've come to meet you.'

'Oh, is it you?' a voice rose as if from a deep, dark cave. 'I, too, have waited for you . . . if I didn't flee like the others, it was because I knew you'd come some day. You didn't look like someone who'd break his word.' In the midst of her sobbing, she muttered, 'Don't I look ugly and disfigured, like a witch?'

Looking compassionately at her, he replied, 'No, if beauty lies in the eye of the beholder, you are still the same Dharmi I saw last time.' He paused. 'Because you have a beautiful soul.'

'Ah, that is the man I fell in love with,' she sighed.

'If my love for you had been physical,' said the Buddha, 'I wouldn't have sought you out here. I always remembered you as my mentor for whom I have great respect.'

Now struggling to gather herself up, Dharmi asked, 'What are you holding in your hand?'

'I've brought you some ointment, which may give you relief, howsoever temporarily.'

As he took out a pinch of the ointment, and tried to apply it to her face, she flinched. 'No, don't touch me. You'll get it too. I'll burn in *naraka* if I let you also catch this deadly disease.'

'No, let me do it,' he insisted, and he began to apply the ointment to her face.

'Let me look at you a little closely,' she said. 'Are you a mortal or a celestial being? Since the plague is for mortals only, maybe you won't catch it. Still . . .' she trailed off. 'Let me tell you what I thought when we last met—that if I didn't have you in this life, I'd certainly get you in the next.'

Smiling, he said, 'But maybe I'd die only once, and then no death for me thereafter.'

'You seem to be talking in riddles,' she said, puzzled. 'Tell me, did you succeed in your mission, whatever it was? That was the excuse you gave me for not staying with me that night.'

The Buddha was impelled to share everything with her. He told her how he spent some time in Uruvala, before moving on to Gaya where he saw the Divine Light.

'Ah, the Buddha!' she exclaimed, riding the crest of an irrepressible emotion. 'You know, a man who came here from Sarnath said something about your first sermon there.' She paused. 'You may be a saviour for the entire world, but you'll always be my love.' Another pause. 'A thousand pities, however, that there's hardly anyone left in this ghost town to listen to you . . .'

'Aren't you audience enough for me?'

Her eyes still glowing with wonder, she said, 'I wish I could proclaim to the world that I knew the Buddha as nobody else would ever know.'

'Indeed,' he said. 'Now, won't you let me stay with you for the night, to let me redeem my pledge?'

'No,' she replied. 'This time, it's me who will ask you to leave as soon as possible. There's death in the air . . . so go away, my darling Buddha, out of this *naraka* . . . But pray for me . . . I'll be thinking of you in my last moments . . .'

'Indeed, I'll pray for you, Dharmi,' he said. 'But don't be afraid of death. It's just like moving from one house to another.'

Before leaving her, he applied some ointment to her face again.

'Since you are a blessed soul, I know no harm will come to you,' she said. 'Still, take care, my love.'

She somehow managed to place her head at his feet, and then she began to cry bitterly.

The Buddha carried this tearful face in his mind as he walked out of Greha.

17

The Budha now wanted to revisit the cremation ground in the forest where he'd spent a few days with the sadhu, his first mentor. It was quite dark by the time he reached the forest.

But as he looked about, there was no sign of the sadhu. Where had he gone? the Buddha wondered. All that he saw there was a heap of skulls. Maybe the sadhu had died, leaving his own skull here. If only each skull could carry its identification on it . . . but death leaves only a handful of ashes to be immersed in some confluence.

Lost in these thoughts, he dozed off under a tree. At dawn, he picked up his bowl and walked over to the pool to get some water. As he dipped it into the pool, he heard a noise in the bushes on the other side. Then a tigress appeared with its cub. But before drinking from the pool, it darted a curious look at the Buddha, who seemed to be a new visitor in the forest. Sensing that the man intended no harm, it drank some water, stretched up leisurely on a patch of grass, and began to lick its cub all over—its head, neck and flanks. Then, as the cub climbed over its mother, and began to suckle at its teats, the tigress closed its eyes as if in supreme bliss. It would take only a year for the cub to grow into adulthood, thought the Buddha, and then its mother would let it go out alone for a hunt, on its own. But would it recognize its mother if they met in the forest, a few years later? Suddenly, an image rose in his mind—Yashodhara watching Rahul grow into adulthood. But would she let him go alone on a 'hunt', on his quest for self-realization?

As he thought of his wife and son, he felt a wrench in his heart. No, that way lay attachment, the source of all pain. He must muster up enough courage to keep himself out of any emotional embroilment. Hadn't Mara also tried to entangle him in the sensual world?

Immersed in these musings, he reached the bank of the river Satya that now seemed to divide two worlds—the one that he had renounced, and the other that he'd seen after his enlightenment under the Bodhi tree.

Suddenly he heard something splash in his stream of thoughts. It was a boat rocking in the swirling waters, as the boatman inside it snored away. As the man heard some footsteps near his boat, he opened his eyes, and there stood in front of him someone in saffron robes, with a brass bowl in his right hand.

'Ah, Prince Siddhartha!' the boatman exclaimed, instantly recognizing him. Then, taking a close look at him, he remarked, 'I knew you'd come home some day. But it's been a long time.' After a pause, he said. 'Let me have the honour to ferry you across the river.'

'But I have nothing to give you this time,' said the Buddha.

'Here is your gold ring, sir,' he responded. 'Good enough for a hundred ferries.'

As the boat touched the other bank, the boatman asked him, 'Do the people here know that you've returned?'

'No,' he replied. 'I'd prefer to enter the city incognito, because I don't want any fanfare on my return.'

Stepping out of the boat, the Buddha started walking towards the front gate of the royal palace. As he was about to walk past it, a guard stopped him. But recognizing him instantly, he cried out, 'Prince Siddhartha!' At once he ran inside, shouting like a man in a frenzy. 'The prince has returned!'

As soon as the news broke, everyone in Kapilavastu rushed towards the front gate. All men, women and children now stood along the streets, waiting to have a glimpse of the Buddha.

But before the crowd could reach the gate, the royal chariot had already arrived there. On seeing the Buddha walking through the gate barefoot, holding a brass bowl in his right hand, King Suddhodana got off his chariot. As he gestured to bow to his son, the Buddha took him in a fervent embrace.

'No, Father, don't embarrass me,' he said, touching his feet. 'I am your son, whatever I may be today. Let me tell you that you were my fellow-traveller all through my spiritual voyage. If you wanted, you could have sent your spies after me to track me down. But you let me be.'

As the Buddha looked around, he became aware of Asita's presence just behind his father. 'May I also take some credit for what I'd prophesied?' intervened the royal priest. Then turning to the king, he said, 'Although you put aside my prediction as mere fantasy, you may now see how it has all come true.' He paused. 'Well, let me make another prophecy. A couple of centuries from now, a great Indian emperor, anguished over mindless killing in a war, will also renounce his throne and become a monk—as an ardent believer in your son's teachings. So, you see, Siddhartha will always be remembered as the King of kings, an uncrowned emperor whose spiritual domain would extend far beyond even Bharatvarsha.'

The Buddha blushed at this compliment. 'I look forward to seeing you alone, O Master,' said the Buddha to Asita, 'some time during my stay here.'

'You'd be welcome any time.'

Then, as he saw Channa, who was standing shyly behind one of the royal counsellors, he walked over to him and hugged him warmly.

'O Channa,' he asked, 'how did you fare all these years? I see you greying at the temples. A long time it's been.'

'Yes, O Prince, I missed you too,' he mumbled, choked with emotion.

'Those, who are closest to me must come last,' he said to Channa. 'Aren't you going to invite me to breakfast in your cottage? Just a bowl of rice and a glass of milk would do.'

'I'd be honoured.'

'How about Kanaka?' the Buddha asked, as the image of his favourite horse rose in his mind.

'Passed away. Just a couple of months after you left. He couldn't bear the pain of separation.'

The Buddha felt as if he'd lost a limb from his body. Carried away by emotion, he asked, 'Where did you bury him?'

'On the bank of the Satya, where you last saw him . . . I dug a deep pit, covered him with a silken cloth . . .' He broke off as he choked.

The Buddha looked sideways to hide his tears.

King Suddhodana didn't wish to intervene in his son's conversation with Channa.

The Buddha then turned to his father and asked, 'Where is she?'

'I did send her word about your return, but she refused to be just one of the crowd. If he is the Buddha for others, she said, he is still my husband, and the father of Rahul. So he must come himself to my palace.'

'Quite understandable,' said the Buddha.

King Suddhodana, then took him in his chariot to the palace he'd gifted to his son on his wedding.

Meanwhile, two faces were looking out of the window of the palace.

'Look out there, Rahul, at that royal chariot,' Yashodhara said, excitement writ large on her face. 'That man in saffron, sitting beside your grandfather—he is your father.'

'Oh, he is so handsome,' exclaimed Rahul.

'Like you,' she said. 'You got it all from him—his looks, his mind and his heart.' She paused. 'This window from where we are both watching him, was his favourite place—to look out for the darkness beyond light . . .'

'This has been my favourite place too—to introspect.'

'Like father, like son,' said Yashodhara, smiling.

The chariot stopped at the gate, and both of them rushed out.

Stepping forward in excitement, Yashodhara touched her husband's feet.

'Oh, my Lord!' she exclaimed. 'After years, of waiting . . .' Then, pointing to Rahul, 'Here is the memento from you . . .'

But the Buddha's eyes were already riveted on the young, handsome face. Rahul, with tears streaming down his cheeks, placed his head on his father's feet. When the Buddha raised him, two pairs of eyes probed each other.

'There was never a moment when I could keep you

out of my mind, dear Father,' said Rahul. 'But I also knew you'd gone away on a mission. So I just prayed for your return, patiently.'

'You know,' intervened Yashodhara, 'he'd also sit under your favourite tree, and meditate for hours together . . . so I never had all of him, any time, the unfortunate creature that I am.'

King Suddhodana listened to every word, although he pretended to be looking sideways at a painting on the wall. Seizing a moment's pause in their conversation, he moved in.

'Let me tell you something, Siddhartha. All these years, Yashodhara never slept in her bed. Always on the bare floor, with no pillow under her head. As regards her food, she took just a bowl of rice with a glass of milk . . . and have you noticed what she is wearing now? A plain cloth saree, and no jewellery . . .'

The Buddha looked compassionately at his wife—daughter of King Suprabuddha and married to the crown prince of Kapilavastu, not a wandering mendicant.

'This was indeed the woman I married,' said the Buddha, 'someone whose sacrifice has been no less painful than mine . . . I bow to her.' He paused. 'I can see how well she has brought up my son . . . in fact, I'm going to ask for alms from her.'

Everyone was frozen in suspense to know what he had in mind. Then holding out his bowl to Yashodhara, he asked,

'O gracious lady, what are you going to drop into my bowl?'

'Anything you wish, my Lord,' came the prompt response.

'Then let me have Rahul,' he said, 'although I have never so far solicited anything of my choice.'

'So you are going to take away even the last prop of my life . . . all right, I'd let you have him. After all, he is your son too.'

But before she could say anything more, Rahul had already put his arms around his father.

'I'll be his disciple,' Rahul said. 'Not for me any worldly glory . . . I also want to reach the heart of darkness, beyond the razzle-dazzle of worldly life.'

'So the bird's already flown out of my hands,' Yashodhara said, light-heartedly. 'Since I knew it was coming, I have no regrets.' She took a deep breath. 'But I also want you to drop something here,' she implored, holding out the hem of her cotton saree.

'Anything I can,' the Buddha responded.

'I also wish to be taken into your fold. Would you take a woman as your disciple?'

'Indeed, you'd be my first nun. Why should there be any discrimination between man and woman? A seeker has no caste, creed, colour—or gender. But I'd like you and Rahul to travel independently, and propagate my message of love and peace to the world.'

At this point, King Suddhodana moved in, his eyes

glowing with pride. 'Would you agree to give a sermon, my son, in Kapilavastu this evening? The entire city would like to hear you.'

'I'd be happy to do it, Father,' the Buddha replied. 'Nothing would give me greater pleasure than to share with my native city what I saw and heard under the Bodhi tree.'

Even at this short notice, the king's chief counsellor, Sukumdev, was able to organize the Buddha's sermon on an open ground, a little distance away from the audience hall.

As soon as the Buddha appeared, followed by the king, Yashodhara and Rahul, the crowd broke into a tumultuous cheer. Asita then led the Buddha to the platform, and introduced him. 'In honouring the Buddha, we are honouring ourselves—our city Kapilavastu, our king, Yashodhara and Rahul. History will recognize that the Buddha was a gift to mankind from this city. As you already know, I've had the privilege of tutoring young Siddhartha. But now I'd be privileged to sit at his feet, and learn how the riddle of human existence could be solved. So, here is Siddhartha, now the Buddha, the King of kings!'

Overwhelmed by his former guru's words, the Buddha rose, greeted the audience with folded hands, and began to speak.

'Fellow citizens of Kapilavastu, I am not the King of kings, but only one of you, a commoner, who will continue to seek and strive. Let me first say that I am delighted to be back home, and to have this opportunity to address you. I will speak in Pali, a language of the common man. Sanskrit is the language of the elitist priests who are afraid of sharing with the common man the truths that lie hidden in our scriptures. But the fact is that divine bliss is attainable not through rituals, nor chanting mantras mindlessly, but through righteous action. Not words but deeds, because words often weave a tangled web in which our mind gets enmeshed.

'Let me begin with the mind which can turn *svarga* into *naraka*, and vice-versa. The mind is a monkey that leaps from one tree to another, from one housetop to another, restlessly. Blessed is the man who can control his mind's vagaries. Let us try to be like a skilled archer who controls his mind before hitting the target. On the other hand, a vagrant mind is like a straw in the wind. Unwise are those who let their thoughts flit about like autumn leaves. More injurious to a man is his own restless mind than the harm done to him by his enemies.

'I have come to believe that it is only through disengagement from worldly embroilments that we can attain peace and happiness. Therefore, a disinterested action, that is action done regardless of any recompense, is the only way to divine bliss. It is only when we are occupied with the future, fearful of the unknown, that we get embroiled in anxiety which saps our energy and pushes us into depression.

'Finally, what matters is the quality of life that we live. A single day of unblemished existence is far more rewarding than a long span of life lived mindlessly.'

Then the Buddha struck a personal note that touched a deep chord in the hearts of his listeners. Looking at the members of his family, sitting in the front row, he said, 'Fortunate is the man who has the support of his family in whatever he chooses to achieve. This is where I have been singularly blessed. You know that I have been away from my family—my father, wife and son—for several years. But since I carried their blessings with me throughout my spiritual voyage, I never faltered or stumbled.

'Much as I'd like to stay back here, I have still miles to go to achieve my goal. My wife and son have already pledged to join me in propagating whatever I've learnt in life. But each of them would go his or her own way, for ultimately every human being has to be on his own.'

As he stopped, a loud cheer rent the air.

'Long live our Buddha!'

'Eternal life to him!'

18

Next morning, when the Buddha knocked at Channa's door, it was his wife who answered it. He heard her whisper to her husband, 'It's the prince.'

When Channa appeared at the door, a little confused, the Buddha said, 'If I have come a little too early, it's because of my eagerness to have a long chat with you. So let's go and sit on the same rock where I announced, years ago, my decision to renounce everything.'

By now it was dawn, and the sun's rays were changing colours from light brown to ochre and deep crimson. Since sunrise always fascinated the Buddha, his eyes lingered for a while on the golden bowl.

Then, turning to Channa, the Buddha asked about Saroja, his daughter.

'She passed away a year ago,' he replied. 'In a sense, death came as a relief to her. She'd suffered too much, too long.'

'I am very sad to hear this. But you took great care of her.'

'We all have to go sooner or later,' Channa sighed. 'But massaging her crippled legs was like praying . . .'

'What about Kanaka? I thought of him quite often, during my travels.'

'Oh, that animal!' Channa exclaimed. 'Unimaginable was his dedication to you. You know, after we parted by the riverside, he stood there, petrified. Since I never whipped him, I just waited for him to move. Parting from you, he staggered several times, as if all energy had drained out of him. Here was a virile stallion, now hobbling like a decrepit old man.'

'Oh!' the Buddha exclaimed, covering his eyes with both hands.

'There's my Buddha, preaching detachment to others but . . .' Channa jibed, light-heartedly.

'Even I cannot claim absolute disengagement, for aren't we humans after all? All we can do is keep moving in that direction.' He broke off. 'Where did you bury him?'

'I loaded him on a bullock cart, carried his body to the same spot by the riverside, dug a grave and laid him to rest.'

'You must have been a sage in your previous life, O Channa. Now you may understand why I have always looked upon you as my divine charioteer, like Krishna.'

Channa blushed.

'Channa, I have often pondered over animals and birds. Strange creatures they are, from whom we can learn so much.' Then he told him how a king cobra lent him a protective cover while he was asleep one night in a forest. And how on his way back he saw, one morning, a tigress letting its cub suckle at its teats as they both lazed on the bank of a pool—a touching scene of family happiness.

'But you left your cub behind when you set out on your voyage,' Channa teased again.

'That was the most agonizing thing I have done. It was like tearing my heart out, and letting it writhe on the ground.' He then lapsed into silence. When he came to, he asked Channa, 'How did my Rahul fare during my absence?'

'You wouldn't believe me if I told you that he endured the separation very stoically. While sages only preach disengagement, he lived it. I used to see him sitting under your favourite tree, meditating for hours. In spite of the king's persistent efforts to engage him in martial sports, he never showed any interest in such activities. He just brooded like a dove, always immersed in introspection. One day, he asked me to take him for a ride through the marketplace. At first I refused, but when he insisted I had to give in. However, unlike you, he didn't ask me any questions—he just observed and sighed. Another day, as I was driving him through the city in the blazing sun, he suddenly asked me to stop. His eyes had caught sight of a sparrow under a tree, gasping for breath. He jumped off the chariot, walked up to the bird, and picked it up in his left hand. Then, carrying it to a little puddle of water close by, he poured some drops down its throat. In a few minutes, the rejuvenated bird focused its eyes on Rahul's face as if it were thanking him. Rahul then caressed its puny body from neck to tail, till it unfurled its feathers and flew away. When he returned to the chariot, he said to me, "I had a little chat with that bird, and each time I asked him something, it responded only with its eyes. I think these birds speak only the language of eyes and gestures . . ." Being a young man of great compassion and sensitivity, how could he take to martial arts?' Then, taking a deep breath, Channa resumed, 'He is your exact replica—the same broad forehead, the same eyes like two deep, brown pools. You once told me that you regretted getting married, wouldn't you have missed a rare jewel like Rahul then?'

'Indeed,' muttered the Buddha.

'When you mentioned in your sermon last evening how your family supported you, it was, in fact, Rahul who was your main prop.'

Now looking directly at Channa, the Buddha said, 'Do you know that Rahul is eager to become a bhikshu—and so is his mother?'

'Lucky man—that's what you are,' Channa said.

'You haven't told me anything about my father, Channa. How did he take my renunciation?'

'It shattered him,' answered Channa. 'He kept himself away from the audience hall for a whole month. And he must have shed a river of tears.'

'Won't you come in for breakfast?' It was Channa's wife, who had been waiting a long time.

'Yes, we'll be there, Supriya,' said Channa.

19

Stepping out of Channa's cottage, the Buddha began to walk up and down the gravel path around the central fountain, near the audience hall. Then sitting on the edge of the fountain, he began to see jets of water spurting up into the air. In the little pool around the fountain, the fish were chasing each other. How long does a fish live, and does it undergo any suffering—sickness or old age? And is there any mourning on the death of a fish? Was longevity of life any criterion of happiness?

As he was lost in these thoughts, he saw an old man emerging from the Shiva temple, a little distance away from the fountain. As the man drew close, a sparkle of recognition appeared in the Buddha's eyes. There was Asita, the royal priest, now old and grey-haired, walking unsteadily. Although the Buddha had talked to him when he entred Kapilavastu, it was only now that he was able to have a close look at him. At once he stood up, and bowed to his old teacher.

'Ah, my Siddhartha,' Asita said, 'but now, the Buddha!' He paused. 'Our roles are now reversed because here I stand before my guru, not my pupil.'

'No, Master,' said the Buddha. 'You'd always remain someone who initiated me into self-realization.'

'That's your graciousness,' Asita said. 'You know, I am now eighty, but one is never too old to learn.' He paused. 'Tell me, how did you attain enlightenment . . . ? I will always take pride in having prophesied that you'd some day be the world's saviour.'

'What I learnt one night, in Gaya,' the Buddha responded, 'was strikingly simple—that the path to enlightenment is just righteous action, not ritualism or theological casuistry.'

For a moment, Asita's brow was knitted as if he were pondering over what the Buddha had just said. Then, with a smile on his face, he remarked, 'How true! You know how most of us get lost in the labyrinth of abstruse theology. A good teacher, I now realize, is one who can make difficult concepts sound simple . . .'

The Buddha flashed a smile at Asita's response.

'Do you believe in soothsaying?' Asita asked.

'Not really,' he replied. 'But hasn't your prediction come true?'

'Let me tell you something you may not know,' said Asita.

'I was the interpreter of the dream your mother had, a little before she delivered you.'

'What was her dream?' the Buddha asked, curiously.

'It was a night in mid-spring, with a gentle breeze soughing through the flower beds. As the sky was cloudless, the moon and the stars seemed to shine in their pristine glory. Suddenly a six-layered star descended from the sky and entered your mother's womb. Its token was a six-tusked elephant, white as milk and chaste as a lotus. As your mother, Queen Mahamaya, awoke out of her dream, she heard a divine melody in the air. Then came the words, "Look and behold, a new messenger will soon arrive. The dead will rise from their pyres; the earth will be reborn, and the solar system will recycle itself." That messenger, I told your father, would be a son born to him. Thus were you born.' As the Buddha kept gazing at Asita, with the curiosity of a doe's eyes, the priest continued, 'Looking perplexed, your father sought some more testimony. I then asked him to look at the thirty-two marks on your body—signs of divinity.' Asita paused. 'When I prophesied that the child was destined to renounce the world to seek nirvana, your father's face went ashen.' Then, taking a deep breath, Asita held the Buddha's hands, and exclaimed, 'And there, sitting beside me now, is the Lord saviour of the world!'

The Buddha rose from the railing, and placed his head at Asita's feet. 'No, Master,' he breathed into the air, 'I am not a saviour, but still a seeker who must continue his spiritual voyage. And that's where I'd need your blessings.'

Asita resumed. 'It seems that your mother came into this world only to deliver a divine child, because she passed away just a week after your birth . . . I'm not sure if you know that you were breastfed by Princess Mahaprajapati, who'd herself delivered a male child, just two days before your birth. Grateful to the princess, your father gifted her a house, just behind the audience hall.'

Dazed and dumbfounded, the Buddha felt as if he were listening to a fairytale.

'So I had two mothers?' the Buddha now broke into words. 'One, my own, and the other my foster mother who was to me like Yashodhara was to Lord Krishna.'

Smiling, Asita said, 'Yes.'

'Of course, I know,' continued the Buddha, 'that I was brought up by some royal maids, but I never knew about my mother, Mahaprajapati.'

Asita then explained how she had to leave Kapilavastu when the Buddha was about ten months old, because her husband had taken up a job elsewhere. But when he died, she chose to return to Kapilavastu. In fact, she was in the city when you were received at the entry gate, and she was excited to know that her little Siddhartha was now the Buddha.

'Then why wasn't she there?'

'Like your wife, Yashodhara, she didn't want to be just

one of the crowd. She now expects you to meet her at her house.'

'She is right,' said the Buddha. 'I must visit her at the earliest. I'm sure I'd be able to recognize her instantly.'

'Surely,' said Asita.

'Where is her house?' he now asked.

'It's a blue single-storey house, just behind the audience hall.'

'What about her own son?' he asked.

'I don't know anything about him,' Asita said. 'She'll tell you everything when you meet her. All I know is that she fed you like her own child, as if you and her son were twins . . .'

So excited was the Buddha that he decided to see her immediately.

20

It was a small house, but with the elegance of a palace—an arched front gate, a tortoise shell-shaped dome, and marble pillars supporting the entire structure. The front gate carried a name carved in sandalwood—'Mahaprajapati.' In front of the house was a luscious lawn with a gravel path leading up to the front door, above which was engraved the gayatri mantra in gilded letters:

Om bhur bhuvah swaha
tat savitur varenyam
bhargo devasya dhimahi
dhiyo yonah prachodayat om

As the Buddha walked through the front gate, two peacocks emerged from behind a pillar. Beautiful birds they were, each with iridescent feathers. But while the male peacock had a rose-coloured tiara, its female partner had an azure crest. While the male bird strutted forth screeching, as if to greet the visitor, its partner ambled behind, demurely. The Buddha caressed both peacocks, lover of birds and animals that he was. He then walked up to the front door. A gentle knock, and the door opened. There stood in front of him his foster mother, Mahaprajapati, draped in a white saree. At once he lay prostrate at her feet.

Raising him up, she exclaimed 'Oh, my son!' with tears of joy streaming down her cheeks. Then, probing his face, she said, 'Of course, I have recognized you—those deep brown eyes, always sparkling with curiosity, and those lips like rose-petals—' She paused. 'But now you've grown so tall and handsome—no longer my little Siddha, but the Buddha. I would have come to the front gate of Kapilavastu to welcome you, but the crowd there . . . I knew, however, that you'd come here to meet me.'

'Like my wife Yashodhara,' he said, 'who also kept away from the crowd, and expected me to meet her at her palace.'

Then, Mahaprajapati led him inside the house.

'A beautiful house, Mother,' he said.

'Gifted by King Suddhodana, for breastfeeding his motherless child.'

'But wasn't I fortunate to have another mother whose milk still runs through my veins, like divine nectar?' He paused. 'Tell me, Mother, what kind of a child I was.'

'Gentle as a dove,' she replied. 'So different from my

own son, Samir. While he'd sometimes bite my nipples, you just suckled gently . . . it was, of course, blissful to have you both, each on either side, like holding the treasurs of both worlds. She paused. 'But while Samir often cried, you were always quiet, your eyes seeking something . . . I should have divined that, like a restless bird, you'd fly away some day. But now the bird has come back to its nest, though, I guess, for a short while only.'

'Where is Samir, Mother dear?' he asked.

'Gone to a small town, Venipet, near Hastinapur. He is a priest there at the Krishna temple.'

'So you lost both of your children to divinity,' he quipped, smiling. 'I think there was something divine in your milk that turned us both away from this mundane world.' He paused. 'Now I know that it was your milk that sustained me all through my wanderings. And, it surely acted as my shield against Mara, who tried to tempt me away from my quest while I was deep in meditation under the Bodhi tree in Gaya.'

'Yes, the whole country knows how you attained enlightenment.'

A brief silence now fell between the two. Then he asked, 'Who carved the gayatri mantra on your front door, Mother?'

'Samir,' she replied. 'Woodcarving was his hobby, and he often hummed the mantra.'

'I learnt the mantra while I was in my mother's womb,' the Buddha said. 'Like Abhimanyu who learnt the secret of the *Chakravyuha* while he was in Subhadra's womb.'

'Amazing!'

'Let me also tell you that I can still recall the orange hem of your saree which covered my face whenever you fed me. I always felt so cool and secure there.'

'Fantastic!' she exclaimed. 'Yes, I often wore sarees with an orange border . . . I marvel at your memory.' She paused. 'I used to cover you with my saree, to protect you from the evil eye.'

'How I wish you'd stayed with me during my childhood and youth. But I learnt from Asita that you had to leave Kapilavastu when I was just a year old.'

'We had to leave as my husband was offered a position elsewhere, in the army. When he was killed in a battle, I felt lonesome and chose to return to Kapilavastu.'

'I am very sad to hear about your husband's death. But that which is born, O Mother, must die . . . In a sense, I am also happy that you are back in Kapilavastu. Otherwise, I would have missed you.'

'Destiny weaves its own intricate pattern,' Mahaprajapati said.

Suddenly, the Buddha's eyes fell on a painting on the wall in front of him.

'Who painted that, Mother?'

'Samir. He painted whenever he was not meditating.'

'I must meet my brother,' he said. 'He must be very handsome.'

'Not as handsome as you,' she countered. 'You were chiselled by the Divine Spirit as a god in human form. Your body carried thirty-two marks, signifying divinity. So wasn't I fortunate to breastfeed a little god?' She smiled.

'But what about the scars on my legs, the boils under my feet, dear mother?' he said. 'It was a very painful pilgrimage, walking barefoot and sleeping on the ground.'

Gently she intervened, 'Strait is the pathway to self-realization.'

'How about you, Mother,' he asked, 'living alone, away from your only child?'

Taking a deep breath, she replied, 'But aren't silence and solitude prerequisites of self-awareness?' She paused. 'Also, I'm not entirely lonely, because there are my friends—those two peacocks. They sing and dance for me. I even let them into my main room . . . so my life flows on like a gentle stream.'

'How true,' the Buddha said. 'Your peacocks are very friendly creatures. They greeted me as I walked through the front gate.'

'They don't do that to every visitor. They must have taken you as someone extraordinary. And, indeed, you are—the Buddha!'

'If there is something special about me, Mother, it's

because of you. I may be the Buddha to others, but for you I'd always be Siddha.'

As she walked him to the front gate, the peacocks came up behind him, expecting him to fondle them again. The Buddha then mumbled to them, 'Will you take care of my mother?'

As Mahaprajapati bade him farewell, her eyes became tearful.

21

Since the Buddha's next destination was Venipet, where he wanted to meet Samir, he saw another long journey in front of him. It was with great sadness that he bade farewell to his family—his wife, son and father. But change and separation, he believed, are inalienable coordinates of human existence. And isn't attachment the primary source of all sorrow and pain? He was happy to see that his family had understood the nature of his mission. So, cheerfully, they let him resume his voyage.

Once again, he wanted to leave Kapilavastu unnoticed, without any fanfare. So he decided to walk away at midnight, with only Channa to accompany him up to the river Satya.

'But no tears this time, Channa,' he said. 'Let it be a happy parting, although we may never meet again.'

As Channa turned his face around to hide his tears, the

Buddha said, 'There you go again . . . but who knows, we may meet again, if not in this world . . .' He broke off. 'I'll pray for you to attain nirvana which you truly deserve.' Something then flashed through his mind. If nirvana was release from the cycle of birth and death, then it should be possible for their two souls to meet again, somewhere in heaven.

The boatman had to be gently touched out of his sleep again. But as soon as he saw the Buddha with his companion, he jumped up, saying, 'How is it, O Prince, that you've not come in your chariot this time?'

'Now I prefer walking,' responded the Buddha. 'But sailing in your boat is different.'

'My pleasure, sir,' the boatman said. Then pointing towards the gold ring on his left hand, he added, 'This should take care of your countless ferries . . .'

'No, friend, this may be the last time . . .'

'Don't say that, O Prince,' the boatman said. 'There's always another time.'

Then waving farewell to Channa, the Buddha stepped into the boat. He saw Channa standing tearfully on the bank till the boat reached the other side of the river.

This time, the Buddha did not walk through the forest; he chose a different route.

It took him a night's walking to realize that he was now in a region quite different from the Indo-Gangetic plain that he'd travelled through earlier. Being a native of Kapilavastu, a city situated at the foot of the Himalayas, he now felt more at home in this northern part of the country, with hills, valleys and rivers—and fields of corn, maize, wheat and sugarcane. Since he wanted to be close to nature, he left the highway and chose to walk along the fields.

He'd hardly walked a little distance along a maize field, when it started to drizzle. As he looked around for some shelter, he saw a man running up to him with a shawl in his right hand. He was a tall, stout man, with broad shoulders and a long beard.

'You'll get drenched, Swamiji,' he said, 'as this drizzle may soon swell into rain.' Pointing to a massive banyan tree, sprawling over a large stretch of ground, he added, 'Come with me, please. It's a tree that has always offered me shelter from rain and the hot sun.' Then, asking the Buddha to cover his head with the shawl, he asked him to follow.

Under the tree, the Buddha saw a woman, bare-headed, with a mat spread on the ground on which some food was laid out.

'I'd taken it off her head, Swamiji, as nothing else came handy.' He paused. 'A woman's extra garment is often a great boon.'

'I don't know how to thank you for your graciousness, dear friend,' said the Buddha.

'On the contrary,' said the man, 'it would be very gracious of you if you'd join us for this meal. A holy man's presence is always a blessing.'

Overwhelmed by the man's hospitality, the Buddha sat down to join the couple. He saw on the mat a variety of dishes—buttered chapatis, various vegetables, curd and a large bowl full of butter milk.

'I notice,' said the Buddha, 'that both of you are vegetarian.'

'Indeed,' he said. 'Isn't it a sin to kill another creature to fill one's own stomach?' Then, pointing towards a corn field, he added, 'When God's soil grows so much fresh food, why go in for dead meat?'

'Absolutely,' replied the Buddha.

'Do bulls, cows and goats eat meat?' continued the man. Pointing towards a bull tied to the trunk of another tree close by, he added, 'That's my bull and it is happy eating maize, grass and jaggery. I even let it drink a bowl of milk now and then.'

As the Buddha looked at the animal, he noticed that its horns were painted with turmeric, and around its neck was a collar with tiny bells.

An image flashed through his mind—of the young bull that was held within an enclosure and shot at by some street urchins. It would have been wounded to death if he hadn't rescued it.

'A handsome bull,' complimented the Buddha.

'I take care of it, Swamiji, because it is a partner in my work. Ploughs my field, carries me back home at the end of the day, and my wife uses its dung as fuel in the hearth.'

'A real partner, indeed,' said the Buddha.

Meal over, the farmer walked to his field and brought a corncob. As he peeled off its green cover, the kernel emerged with glossy strands that looked like the silken hair of a fairy. And from underneath it appeared the grains of corn, shining like pearls. Peeling off a grain and pressing it between his index finger and thumb, he let its milk ooze out.

'Behold nature's bounty, Swamiji, here's something to both eat and drink.'

His wife then collected some dry twigs from under the banyan tree, roasted the corn and offered it to their guest.

'Thank you, sister,' said the Buddha. He now decided to accept anything offered to him by this couple.

'Come with us, Swamiji,' said the farmer, 'since our village is only three miles away, and the road is quite wet.' As the Buddha got onto their cart, he noticed that the farmer didn't hold any whip or stick in his hands.He just clicked his tongue or gently patted his bull's flanks, whenever he wanted it to run faster.

'My bull likes the jingle of the bells round its neck as it gallops,' the farmer said. 'Of course, I too, sometimes sing to help it beguile the tedium of pulling a cart.'

Indeed, he broke into a song, while his wife started clapping her hands to bring up the beat. It was not a love song but a folk song that glorified Mother Earth for her bounties.

If the birds warble their paeans to you.
O Mother Earth, why shouldn't I?
Countless bounties are hidden in your womb—
gold, diamonds, iron and water.
But, above all, the vegetation
that sustains my body.
A seed planted in the soil,
and you nurture it into a stalk of maize,
corn, paddy or wheat.
If the sky cannot quench a tree's thirst
there's enough water in your womb
to make up for it.

I know that at the end of the day,
I will return to you,
dust unto dust.

But it is my wish, O Mother Earth,
that my ashes be not immersed in any confluence,
but blown away by the wind, over some field,
to nurture a seed into a sapling.

Listening to the song, the Buddha was transported into a different world. How much wisdom was packed into this folk song, he wondered. Did this farmer need to be initiated into any divine doctrine, when he was already there? He was certain that this farmer had already caught the blue bird of happiness, since what sustained him in his life were peace and contentment.

When he pulled up the cart in front of his house, his 15-year-old son came running up to greet his parents.

'Did you get wet on the way, Father?' he asked.

'No, we started only after the drizzle stopped,' the farmer replied.

Even before the farmer asked his son to bow to the swami, he'd touched the Buddha's feet. Caressing his head, the Buddha asked, 'Do you go to any gurukul, young man?'

But the farmer moved in to explain that his son went to a little school in the village itself, run by a pandit.

'I didn't want to send him to Lalwani, a town just about two miles away. These towns, Swamiji, sow greed and reap misery.'

'A wise decision,' said the Buddha.

'In any case, he will have to follow our ancestral profession, farming,' said the farmer.

As they were talking, someone showed up at the house.

'I came to say that there'll be no school today as I'll be away to see a sick friend in Lalwani.'

'This is Pandit Kishorilal,' said the farmer to the Buddha. 'He runs the school.'

The pandit greeted the Buddha with folded hands. Then, looking at him curiously, he asked if he'd be staying in the village for a while.

'No, Panditji, I must move on today itself,' said the Buddha.

'Where have you come from, Swamiji?' he asked.

'Kapilavastu,' answered the Buddha.

'Then you must have met the Buddha there,' he said. 'I have a relative in Lalwani who has heard a great deal about this sage. He now travels all over the country, propagating his message of love and peace.'

Buddha just smiled. Who was this stranger? he wondered. As a divine sparkle appeared in the Buddha's eyes, the pandit asked, 'Are you the Buddha, O Swamiji?'

When the Buddha nodded his head and smiled, the pandit turned to the farmer and said, 'O Ramdev, it's God himself who has spent a day with you. He is the Buddha, the King of kings!'

Instantly, they all fell at his feet, asking for his blessings.

'How could I know,' stuttered Ramdev, 'that the gods sometimes descend from *indraloka* to mingle with mortals . . . ? O Lord, would you, please, forgive me if I said or did anything improper?'

'On the contrary it was a pleasure to be with you, O friend,' said the Buddha. I have learnt so much from you . . . my blessings will always be with you and I'll pray for a bumper crop for you.'

When Ramdev offered to take the divine guest in his cart to any place he wanted to go next, the Buddha said, 'No, please, from this point onwards, I must be on my feet.'

22

En route to Venipet, near Hastinapur—where Samir was a priest at the Krishna temple—the Buddha decided to stop for a day at Kurukshetra, the legendary city. As he was passing through a forest, a couple of miles away from the city, he heard a great commotion ahead of him. A fight was raging between two tribal groups, each armed with spears, bows and arrows. When he asked an elderly tribal what it was all about, he was told that it was a family feud over a large tract of the forest, each side claiming it as its ancestral property.

'So, there's another Kurukshetra going on here,' quipped the Buddha. 'Maybe there's something in the soil here that breeds fighting.'

The man responded, 'How true! Both sides are determined to fight it out till one of them is wiped out.'

'Very sad,' said the Buddha. Then something flashed

through his mind and he walked up to the open space between the two warring groups. As the tribals saw a saffron-robed sadhu, with just a brass bowl in his right hand, they held back their bows and arrows. But suddenly a shout rent the air. It was Mullapati, one of the tribal chiefs. 'Get away, O Swami!'

'A madcap he seems to be,' yelled Bhoollapati, the other tribal chief.

But the Buddha didn't move at all. He just kept looking at the tribal chiefs, his eyes glowing. Then he broke into words, 'Why don't you shoot me down . . . ? Surely, I can't defend myself with just a brass bowl. So go ahead.'

What was the man up to? wondered both the tribal chiefs. Here was a man, armless but defiant, standing there like a statue.

Then, brandishing his bow above his head, Mullapati advanced menacingly towards him. Smiling, the Buddha said, 'That's a mighty weapon you're holding in your hand. May I also try it, please?'

Taking him for a crazy man, Mullapati glowered, 'Have you ever seen a bow?'

'But it's never too late to learn archery,' responded the Buddha, smiling. 'Why don't you let me try?'

The Buddha's strategy was to hold the chief in a brief conversation, to cool down the tempers of the fighting tribals. Bhoollapati now also walked up to the spot to know what his adversary was saying to the sadhu.

Meanwhile, the Buddha was holding Mullapati's bow, and aiming it at a mango tree, quite some distance away.

'May I try to get that raw mango hanging by a slender stem, on top of that tree? Or, should it be just the stem and not the fruit?'

Here was a mad man who was trying to fool them, thought both tribal chiefs.

'You are talking of the stem, when you may not be able to hit even the tree's trunk.'

But the arrow had already whizzed out. And there fell on the ground a raw mango, with its stem snapped in the middle.

Both Mullapati and Bhoollapati were stunned to see this amazing feat of archery. They remained dumbfounded for quite a while. Then Mullapati said, 'That was a marvel, indeed. Are you a wandering mendicant or a gifted archer?'

The Buddha responded, 'Does it matter who I am, dear friend? But, unlike you both, I'd never use a bow to settle disputes.' He paused. 'If you have a problem between yourselves, why don't you sit down and talk?' There was another pause after which the Buddha asked, 'Do you realize that there is also a third party to this feud?'

This confused both Mullapati and Bhoollapati. What was the sadhu up to? they wondered.

'I mean the animals and birds,' resumed the Buddha, 'who also live in the forest. They can also claim it as their ancestral land. So, friends, why don't you try to find an amicable solution, without fighting?'

Hardly had the Buddha stopped speaking when a dark, long-haired tribal emerged from the crowd, and exclaimed, 'Ah, the Buddha!'

Taken aback, the Buddha asked him who he was.

'I was in Magadha some time back to attend a wedding,' he said, 'when King Bimbisara arranged a sermon by you. Then, turning to the tribal chiefs, he added, 'Here is the crown prince of Kapilavastu who would have inherited his father's throne if he had not renounced it all. But, now, he is the Lord saviour of us all—the Buddha!' Saying this, he fell at his feet. A hush fell all around him. 'Why don't you arbitrate between us, O Lord,' now pleaded Mullapati, bowing to the Buddha. A long silence followed. Then spoke the Buddha, his eyes glowing with happiness.

'Why don't you consider dividing the forest equally between the two of you?' he suggested. 'Let peace and amity prevail in your hearts, not hostility which always impoverishes the soul.'

Bowing their heads to the Buddha, both tribal chiefs now agreed to settle their dispute.

When word went around that the Buddha was in Kurukshetra, he was requested to give a sermon later that evening. He chose to speak on peace, compassion and non-violence. But during the day, he walked about the city that had been the battleground of a devastating war between the

Kauravas and Pandavas. He saw visitors pouring into the city, imagining its soil still soaked in the blood of countless soldiers who perished in that war.

In the afternoon, the weather turned turbulent, with lightning and thunder, followed by rain. But, surprisingly, as the afternoon deepened into evening, calm descended all over the city. This enabled the citizens to come out and listen to the Buddha.

As the Buddha climbed up an improvised platform, he noticed in the front row, both Mullapati and Bhoollapati. When they bowed to him, he responded with a smile.

'I propose to speak this evening on a subject which may carry a special message for everyone in this city—violence. Why is man prone to killing fellow human beings, animals and birds? When death is beyond our control, why should we assume the role of arbiters, destroyers and not creators?

'When we raise a sword or bow to kill someone, we forget that our adversary may also kill us. Here on the soil of this historical city was fought a war that let a river of blood flow for eighteen days. There was a mindless massacre of countless soldiers, which left women widowed and children orphaned. It brought the entire Bharatvarsha to the brink of total annihilation. It was a war in which the victorious lost as much as the vanquished.

'It may sound blasphemous, but I must say that Lord Krishna's exhortation to Arjuna to unleash his bow and arrows, even for a just cause, was unjustified. We cannot hold hostages to any end. Perhaps the Lord should have tried harder still to bring both sides to dialogue. So it pains me to imagine him inciting Arjuna to kill his relatives, friends and teachers. The stark truth about any war is that it brings out the worst in man—hatred, anger and revenge.

'Just as the war of Kurukshetra exposed the chinks in such noble warriors as Yudhishthira, Arjuna, Drona and even Krishna, so does violence in any form expose our ugly face. Like lust—man's darkest sin—violence and anger are no less sinful. We are then like a log of wood that is carried away by a tidal wave. Or we are like a rudderless boat at the mercy of a fierce storm.

'Aren't we worse than animals when we engage ourselves in a war? They don't array themselves in any battle formation, nor forge strategies to take the enemy by surprise. They neither wield any weapons of destruction nor seek shelter behind a shield.

'I believe that all feuds can be resolved through peaceful means. Let us vanquish hatred with love, and belligerence with compromise and forgiveness. There is a flame of divinity burning in every human heart. Let us not allow any gust of violence to extinguish it. Let peace prevail on this earth. Let us not forget that we are born human beings, as the crown of creation, and it is our duty to justify this by abjuring violence in every form.

'Finally, let me say that violence can be both verbal and

physical. If one can behead another with one stroke of the sword, one may also hurt with a word of abuse. In fact, a foul tongue is often more lethal than even a sword. So let our hand and tongue speak only the language of peace, love and compassion.'

A silence descended all over the place as the Buddha concluded his sermon. Both tribal chiefs, Mullapati and Bhoollapati, were the first to come to the dais to touch his feet.

'O Lord,' said Mullapati, 'your sermon was an eye-opener. You'd be happy to know that we both have settled our dispute. While the eastern half of the forest will go to Bhoolla, I'll take the western half.'

'I'm delighted to hear this,' responded the Buddha. 'You see, how my bow has worked the other way. Instead of killing anyone, it has brought two estranged hearts together.'

Bhoollapati then asked, 'Are you likely to stay in Kurukshetra for a little while?'

'No,' replied the Buddha. 'I must leave tomorrow morning. But I may stop here for a day on my way back.'

'That's good news,' said Bhoollapati. 'Maybe you'd be gracious enough to spend some time with us in the forest.'

'That's a promise,' assured the Buddha. 'Incidentally, I always feel more at home in a forest than in a city.'

There was a brief silence after which Mullapati quipped, 'By that time, the raw mango you targeted will have ripened.

So you may eat it yourself at a tribal dinner we'll arrange in your honour.'

'Certainly,' said the Buddha, smiling, and walked away.

23

As he walked out of Kurukshetra, and took the road to Hastinapur, he noticed that there were hardly any green fields on either side of the path. Since there were trees all along the way, he found it comfortable walking in their shade to protect himself from the heat of the sun.

But whenever he stopped, in some village or town, he received warm hospitality—food, water and shelter. When he was only a few miles away from Hastinapur, he saw a funeral procession passing by. While the men looked sorrowful, the women were beating their breasts and wailing. When the Buddha wanted to know who'd died, he was told that it was a boy of seven who had drowned in a lake.

'But why this grieving?' the Buddha asked.

The man glowered at the Buddha for being so callous about the death of a young boy.

'Are you out of your mind, O Swami?' he retorted. 'Here we are, plunged in grief, and you sound so insensitive.'

'Indeed, I must apologize,' said the Buddha. 'All that I meant was that if we are blessed with the birth of a child, which is an unexpected gift, why should we raise a hue and cry when that gift is taken away for reasons beyond our comprehension?'

Although the Buddha's words set the man thinking, he responded, 'I say it again that this is not the moment to preach, but to empathize with someone's grief.' He paused. 'Let me tell you that I am the child's paternal uncle. So, please . . .' he trailed off. 'Sometimes I think that you swamis relish talking like gods, not humans.' There was another pause. 'Are you married, O Swami—and if you are, then do you have a son?' The man's pungent rejoinder shook up the Buddha who now thought of Rahul.

'Yes, dear friend, I'm married,' the Buddha responded, gently. 'And I have a son too. Would you still accuse me of being callous and inhuman?'

'O God!' exclaimed the man. 'Then I seek your forgiveness, and I'll remember what you said earlier.'

Since the procession was now nearing the cremation ground, the man felt curious to know who this swami was.

'Who are you, Swamiji?' the man asked.

'I'm just a wandering mendicant,' replied the Buddha.

But the man kept staring at him, puzzled. For once, the Buddha thought he should let the truth out.

'Have you heard about the Buddha?' he asked, flashing his enigmatic smile.

'Ah, the Buddha!' the man exclaimed. 'Who hasn't heard about you, O Lord? We have a bhikshu in our village who is one of your ardent disciples.' The man then fell at the Buddha's feet.

The Buddha now resumed his journey towards Hastinapur. As he approached the Jumna, he saw a boat with some passengers sitting in it. Looking at the Buddha, the boatman said, 'You may also come in, Swamiji—and no fare for you.'

'It's very kind of you,' said the Buddha, as he sat in front, close to the boatman.

As the boat was about to sail away, three more passengers showed up, and requested to be taken on board. Although the boat was quite full, the boatman let them in.

'Aren't you overloading, O boatman?' said an old man, sitting in the rear. 'What if the boat capsizes in the middle of the river?'

'Nothing will happen,' assured the boatman. 'The weather is calm, and so is the Jumna. We'll make it to the other bank, safely. So don't worry.'

Another passenger, sitting next to the old man, whispered into his ears. 'Is he drunk or greedy?'

The boat now lurched into motion, and it began to sail smoothly, like a swan gliding on a lake. The early morning sun, now up on the horizon, began to scatter its gold all over the Jumna. Its reflection in the water looked like a bronze disc.

The Buddha was fascinated to watch the boatman plying the oars, which rose and dipped into the water, rhythmically. Hardly had the boat gone halfway deep into the river when a strong wind rose, and swept across the water, causing soaring waves. But the boatman, with his hands steady on the oars, was like a falconer holding the string tightly to control his bird's flight.

Two women, sitting in the middle of the boat, were busy chatting. The woman with a mole on her left cheek, said to her companion, 'Isn't that swami strikingly handsome? There he is, his face glowing like the early morning sun, and his long curly hair cascading down his shoulders.' She paused. 'I guess he is a virgin, although I have heard of sadhus . . .' she broke off.

'Have you fallen for him?' asked her companion. 'I can see saliva dripping from your mouth. Why don't you invite him to your house in Venipet, if he has no place to stay there?'

Smiling, the other woman sighed, 'That would be a dream come true, but if he chooses to stay at a temple, I wouldn't mind being his devadasi—to keep him company at night after the bells stop chiming and even the deities doze off.'

'A lovely fantasy, but fragile like a rainbow,' quipped the other woman.

Suddenly, as the wind swelled into a storm, all the passengers panicked.

'O Krishna, help us . . .' cried out the old man.

'Let's not worry,' said another passenger. 'We have a skilled boatman who will somehow steer us through.'

But fear seized the passengers when they saw the boatman losing his grip on the oars. The Buddha noticed that his eyes were half-shut as if he were slowly lapsing into a coma. Was it a stroke of dizziness? he wondered. It was time to act when the Buddha saw the man suddenly swoon. Instantly, he grabbed the oars, and braced himself to confront a wave that was about to rock the boat. While the passengers started crying, the Buddha held the oars tightly in his hands and continued to row steadily. He was himself amazed at his skill in controlling the boat.

'That swami will certainly ferry us safely across the Jumna, like Vasudeva,' said a passenger, 'carrying his divine babe, Krishna, to safety.'

His words injected some hope in the other passengers who saw the boat negotiating its way through the turbulent waters. As for the Buddha, his eyes were glued to the oars. He recalled himself as the archer whose arrow had hit the black dot on the cowry, scoring over his rivals—Nanda, Arjuna and Devadatta.

When the boat touched the other bank, everyone saw the boatman still lying unconscious. The Buddha asked the passengers to step out one by one, gently, so as not to rock the boat. As they all trooped out, they waited for their saviour to come out so that they could fall at his feet as a gesture of their gratitude. But the Buddha stayed back for a while to revive the boatman. He scooped up a palmful of water and sprinkled it on his face. Slowly the man opened his eyes, as if awakening after a nightmare.

'Where am I?' he asked the Buddha, dazed.

'We have arrived at the other bank, dear friend,' said the Buddha.

Gathering himself to his feet, the boatman asked, 'Who rowed the boat across the river?'

'I did it,' replied the Buddha. 'When I saw you drop off, I took over.'

'But you are a swami, not a boatman.'

Smiling, the Buddha quipped, 'Maybe I am both. I watched you ply the oars for quite some time, and that was enough for me.' He paused. 'You know, I am a good learner.'

'Indeed, you are,' said the boatman.

'May I ask you something, dear friend? Did you ever have such a stroke earlier?'

'Never,' came the prompt answer. 'But, last night, I had three drinks too many—my cursed addiction to liquor . . . I seek your forgiveness, Swamiji . . . imagine what would have happened if I had not taken you on board.'

'But you must now realize that a boatman has great responsibility on his shoulders,' said the Buddha. 'So many lives to save or let perish . . .'

Hanging his head in shame, the boatman murmured, 'I promise never to touch liquor again.'

'I'm so pleased to hear that,' said the Buddha.

When all the passengers now lay prostrate at his feet, the old man said, 'O Lord saviour, may God bless you!'

'Indeed I need your blessings,' the Buddha responded. As he was about to walk away, the young woman, with the mole on her cheek, asked him, 'Do you have a place to stay in Venipet, Swamiji?'

'Yes, I have come here to meet my brother, who is a priest at a local temple.'

Frustrated, the woman said, 'Oh, I see,' and saw the Buddha walking away towards the town.

24

As the Buddha entered Venipet, he noticed that it was a small town, with several Krishna, Rama, Hanuman and Shiva temples, whose domes and spires glittered in the sunlight. He learnt that it had become a legendary place, because Krishna supposedly stayed here for a day on his way to Hastinapur where he was to plead for peace on behalf of the Pandavas. It was, therefore, the Krishna temple, which had become the most popular place of worship, not only for the local residents but also for pilgrims from all over the country. No wonder that most of the shops in Venipet sold puja flowers and pictures of Krishna—pictures of his childhood and his youth. But he was surprised to notice that there were hardly any pictures of Krishna, exhorting Arjuna to fight on the battlefield of Kurukshetra. Maybe this was because in the popular imagination he was a god who, as a small boy, stole handfuls of butter from his foster mother's matkas, sprinkled rose water at young gopikas, or entertained them with his flute. So which one of the two Krishnas was real for Venipet, the Buddha asked himself—the playful, handsome young Krishna, or the yogi who advocated righteous action, regardless of the reward.

The Buddha had no difficulty in locating the Krishna temple where he hoped to meet Samir. It was an architectural marvel, with a gold-plated cupola and a dome designed in the shape of a tortoise. Encountering a priest at the front gate, he asked him about Samir.

'Indeed, he's there in the temple as one of us. But since today he is observing *mona vrata*, you may have to wait till tomorrow morning.' Then, looking at the Buddha, he asked, 'Are you related to him?'

'He's my brother, and I have come all the way from Kapilavastu to meet him.'

'In that case,' said the priest, 'you may go to his cottage in the rear of the temple, and send in a chit announcing your arrival.'

Before going to the cottage, the Buddha chose to look around the temple. While in the sanctum sanctorum stood a large gold-plated idol of Krishna, poised on his left foot, with a flute at his lips, in the courtyard just outside, sat devotees singing bhajans in praise of the Lord. On the walls of the temple were murals depicting several scenes from Krishna's childhood and youth.

After going around the temple, he walked over to Samir's

cottage. Here he was stopped by a young priest who said brusquely, 'He is not available today, Swamiji.' Even when he told the priest that he was Samir's brother, it didn't work on him.

'Brother, father or uncle, he cannot be disturbed,' said the priest, 'when he is on *mona vrata* and is deep in meditation . . . if you are also a priest, you should understand it better yourself. Can't you wait till tomorrow morning? You may sleep anywhere in the open courtyard here.'

Though hurt and humiliated, the Buddha answered calmly, 'Indeed, I can wait. And, please, forgive me for my impatience.'

Walking around the temple, he chose a quiet spot in the eastern wing to rest. But sleep eluded him because of the chanting of mantras and chiming of bells. A couple of priests, one squint-eyed and the other with bushy eyebrows, kept droning away slokas in the courtyard till midnight, while a small crowd of men and women sat listening intently, their eyes half-shut.

Suddenly, at the stroke of midnight, the temple went mute as if it were now time for even Lord Krishna to have a brief spell of sleep, before the chanting resumed the next morning. As the Buddha stretched himself on the floor behind a pillar and dozed off, he heard some whispering from another pillar close by. Lying on the floor, he noticed from the corner of his eyes, the squint-eyed priest kissing a young woman who seemed to be a devadasi at the temple.

She uncovered her breasts, which the priest began to fondle.

Shocked and outraged, the Buddha leapt to his feet, and the woman hurriedly covered herself and vanished behind a wall surrounding the sanctum sanctorum. Appalled by the scene, he walked up to the priest and said, 'Isn't it a sacrilege to indulge in such misconduct right under the eyes of your deity?'

Brazen and unperturbed, the priest shot back, 'We weren't doing anything, O Sadhu . . . She is a devadasi, who just lay at my feet, asking for my blessing.'

The Buddha realized that he was pitted against a man who was morally too depraved to be reclaimed to probity. Before he could say anything more, the priest also vanished. But the Buddha still stood there, petrified.

Then his eyes caught Krishna's idol in the sanctum sanctorum, gleaming in the light of an earthen lamp. At its feet lay heaps of rose petals and fruits, offerings from the devotees. Since there was now nobody around, rats had emerged from every nook and corner to nibble at the fruits. A rat, the fattest of them all, even jumped onto the idol's head, and perched itself securely on its left shoulder.

Poor Lord Krishna, mused the Buddha, was helpless against these mice which had invaded his domain. This was the stark face of orthodox religion, hidden from the public eye. If Samir's priest had not turned him away, wouldn't he have missed it all? He then surmised how the priests at the temple would react if he delivered a sermon here on the Four Noble Truths. Indeed, this place was beyond redemption.

A doubt now rose in his mind. If this place was irretrievably depraved, how had Samir survived? Or was he also made of the same stuff as the others? Maybe that priest wanted to shield his master who was also with a devadasi inside his cottage. But, instantly, he dismissed this thought. How could Samir, fed on his mother's divine milk, transgress into lust?

As he was walking towards Samir's cottage, he saw a sweeper cleaning the front yard of the temple. Although dark-complexioned and dressed in a soiled dhoti and kurta, he looked exceedingly handsome—broad forehead, thick long hair falling on his shoulders, deep brown eyes and delicate lips. So deeply absorbed was he in sweeping that the Buddha had to cough to attract his attention. Turning around, the sweeper saw someone in a saffron robe, with a brass bowl in his hands. Taking him for a sadhu, he knelt down to his knees, but did not touch his feet.

'Namaskaram, Swamiji,' he said, in a gentle voice.

'I thought you'd also touch my feet,' said the Buddha, smiling.

'But I am an untouchable. So how dare I pollute your body?'

The Buddha not only held his right hand in a firm grasp, but also hugged him fervently.

'There, you see, I have not only polluted my hands but

also my entire body,' said the Buddha, smiling again. 'Why should there be any barrier between human beings? Since birth is only an accident, does it matter if one is born a Brahmin or a Shudra?'

Utterly surprised, the sweeper just kept staring at the Buddha in awe.

'Was it a hallucination, O Swamiji?' he stuttered, as he lay prostrate at the Buddha's feet.

'Why don't you do this cleaning during the day, and not at this unearthly hour?' asked the Buddha.

'Because I am not supposed to be visible during temple hours,' he replied. 'So I do this work when nobody is around.'

The Buddha looked puzzled.

'Do you know the priests here well enough?' the Buddha asked.

'Not really,' the sweeper replied.

'I mean, do you see them with devadasis after the devotees are gone?'

'Maybe I see them indulging . . .' the sweeper broke off.

'Are you married?' asked the Buddha.

'Yes, Swamiji.'

'Any children?'

'Two sons, both teenagers,' he responded.

'Do they go to any gurukul?'

'No, Swamiji,' said the sweeper. 'Who'd let them into any school? So they also do cleaning at night. One at the Rama temple and the other at the Shiva. They have to work to support the family.'

Smiling, the Buddha quipped, 'So all the moral filth in these temples is swept clean by your family.'

Before the conversation could go any further, the sweeper picked up his broomstick and resumed his work. So duty was more important than engaging himself in conversation, the Buddha understood.

'But nobody is watching you now, dear friend,' said the Buddha. 'All the priests and devotees are gone, and even Lord Krishna seems to have dozed off in the sanctum sanctorum.'

'No, Swamiji, the Lord is ever vigilant . . . I feel his presence even when nobody else is around.'

'You are a true devotee, dear friend,' the Buddha said. 'What do you think of Swami Samir? Is he like the other priests?'

Instantly, the sweeper's face brightened. 'He is like a lotus in a dirty pond.' Then, holding his broomstick firmly in his hands, he resumed his work.

Before walking away, the Buddha said, 'I should apologize for coming in the way of your duty.'

'No, Swamiji,' he responded, 'I propose to put in an extra half hour to make up for the time lost . . . but let me say, Swamiji, that when you held me in your arms, I was transported into *svarga*.'

As the Buddha turned towards Samir's cottage, he said

to himself, 'Here was someone engaged in righteous action, without knowing anything about the Four Noble Truths.' As Samir's junior priest was nowhere around, he gave a gentle knock on the door. There now stood in front of him a man of his own age and height, his eyes shining like stars. The Buddha had already recognized the mole on his left cheek that had often fascinated him whenever they both lay in the same crib.

'Brother Samir, can you recognize me?' asked the Buddha, excited to see someone who was breastfed by the same woman.

'No, Swamiji,' came the answer. 'You'll have to tell me who you are.'

'I'm Siddha, King Suddhodana's son, who was nursed by your mother. May I, therefore, call myself your "milk brother" if not your real brother?'

'No longer Siddha, but the Buddha!' exclaimed Samir, 'the Lord saviour of Bharatvarsha.' But when he knelt to touch his feet, the Buddha stepped back, saying, 'Don't embarrass me, dear brother.'

'Indeed you are my brother,' said Samir. 'Oh, how much I used to hear about you from my mother after we migrated to Selwan, where my father became an officer in the royal army. Mother was shattered when my father was killed in a battle. You know, it was I who advised her to return to Kapilavastu to live in the house your father gifted us.'

'Yes, she told me something about it when I met her

in Kapilavastu, a little while ago,' the Buddha said. 'When I learnt from her that you were at the Krishna temple in Venipet, I decided to come here.'

Samir then led him inside his cottage, and asked him to sit on a cot.

'Let me fix you some breakfast, brother,' said Samir. 'I am a very good cook, and we'll talk over the meal.'

In a few minutes, Samir was back in the room with a trayful of rice, and two bowls of milk. Glancing at the food, the Buddha said, 'Looks good. You are indeed a very good cook. For the first time I feel as if I'm going to eat at home.' Then he asked Samir, 'Are you happy at this temple?'

'Is it a temple or a brothel?' came the tart response. 'You'd be shocked to know what goes on here every night . . . if I have become most unpopular here, it's because I've told them off several times.' He paused. 'Incidentally, that young man at my door is not a priest, but my jailor.'

'He told me yesterday,' said the Buddha, 'that since you were on a *mona vrata*, I must cool my heels till morning.'

'He is a liar,' he retorted. 'I am a loner here and, of course, I spend most of my time in meditation.'

'I did tell him that you were my brother, but he still turned me away.'

'Very unfortunate,' Samir said. 'So now you understand my predicament.' He paused. 'I think of my mother quite often, and I send her a message whenever any pilgrim comes here from Kapilavastu. But I've had no contact with her for the last couple of months. I wonder how she is faring . . .'

The Buddha then told him that he spent some time with her during his last visit there. 'It was she who told me that you could be contacted in Venipet, at this Krishna temple.'

'She must be very lonesome,' Samir sighed.

'No,' said the Buddha, 'because she has two peacocks to keep her company.'

A brief silence fell between the two. Then Samir said, 'She doesn't know that I have done a lot of travelling in this part of the country, meeting sadhus and priests. I landed up here because the Bhagavadgita has been a source of great comfort to me.'

'So we've both been voyagers through life,' said the Buddha. 'I think there was something divine in our mother's milk that sent us both wandering about like mendicants.'

'Absolutely,' said Samir.

'But when you chose to stay at this temple, did you get any closer to the Bhagavadgita and Lord Krishna?' asked the Buddha. 'Here the Lord seems to be busy playing with his gopikas.'

The Buddha then shared with him what he saw the previous night in the courtyard, right in front of the sanctum sanctorum.

'Well, that priest,' said Samir, 'didn't have to do it in the open, because most priests here sleep with devadasis in their cottages.'

'Shocking!' exclaimed the Buddha.

There was a long pause in their conversation. Then Samir said, 'Although I have heard a lot about you from the pilgrims coming here from Magadha, Uruvala and other places, I now wish to hear from you directly how you attained enlightenment at Gaya.'

Briefly, the Buddha told him how he saw the Divine Light after a long spell of meditation, but not without a long session with Mara, the tempter. 'But, finally, he had to leave me, crestfallen.' Then the Buddha told him how the Divine Spirit unfolded to him the Four Noble Truths, and the eight-fold path to nirvana. After a brief pause, he also told him about his encounter with the sweeper at the temple.

'Here was someone who didn't need to know anything about the Four Noble Truths,' the Buddha said, 'because he was already there—doing his duty righteously. Incidentally, he holds you in great esteem.'

'His name is Namiaha,' said Samir. 'A wonderful human he is. You know, if I had the power, I'd have made him the High Priest of this temple. But, here, even his shadow is considered profane.'

Samir then went deep into introspection, his eyes half-shut, his forehead knitted. When he came to, he spoke in a voice, tender but resolute.

'You have shown me a new vision of life, brother. I have just resolved to return to Kapilavastu and set up a monastery there to propagate your dharma.'

The Buddha responded with just a kiss on his forehead.

'So my visit here was not entirely fruitless,' said the Buddha, his eyes glowing with happiness. 'In Kapilavastu, you could also take care of your mother, and my father. As for my wife, Yashodhara, and my son, Rahul, they may already be on the road, propagating my message of love, peace and compassion.'

After a brief silence, Samir suggested, 'If you have not planned to go elsewhere so soon, why don't you spend the night with me. Nothing would make me happier.' Then, pointing towards the cot, he said, smiling, 'I'd then imagine it as the crib in which we used to lie together.' A pause. 'I was told by mother that while I was a cry baby, you were always mute like a statue.'

'It was in that crib, Samir,' said the Buddha, ' that I used to look at the mole on your left cheek—the mole that helped me recognize you the moment you appeared at the door. Yes, of course, I'll stay with you tonight, dear brother. And let's sleep alongside each other in that cot to recapture our childhood.'

Overwhelmed, Samir dropped his head on the Buddha's lap, his eyes wet with moisture.

Next morning, Samir walked him to the bank of the Jumna, where the boatman recognized the Buddha instantly.

'Come in, Swamiji,' he said excitedly. 'There will be no overloading this time. Also, I have given up liquor, forever.'

'That's wonderful!' said the Buddha.

Then, turning to Samir, he told him how he'd rowed the boat across the river when the boatman had passed out.

Suddenly, Samir grew emotional and started crying.

'When will I see you again, my brother?' he asked tearfully.

'We may not be able to meet again, Samir . . . but does it matter? Remember that attachment is the source of all sorrow, because change and separation always bring suffering in their wake.'

Samir kept standing by the riverside till the boat vanished deep into the Jumna.

25

It was a smooth sail across the Jumna—no storm or rain. While the passengers were busy chatting, the boatman started humming a folk song about the Jumna, Ganga and Saraswati. Since the Buddha was sitting next to him he listened closely to the song, which described Vasudeva, Krishna's father, carrying the divine babe across the river, with a cobra's hood shielding it from wind and rain. When he finished singing, the Buddha asked him, 'Do you believe in the mythical Saraswati that is supposed to flow underneath the Jumna and the Ganga?'

'Indeed,' he replied.

'But maybe it's just a figment of our imagination as nobody has seen that river.'

'Belief, Swamiji, is a matter of faith. What moves the heart is always something that is invisible and intangible.'

Here was someone, thought the Buddha, who was endowed with innate wisdom.

'I agree, dear boatman,' said the Buddha. Then he added, 'Have you visited the Krishna temple in Venipet?'

'Only once,' he replied. 'But it wasn't a happy experience. 'Crowds, bhajan singing and chiming of bells—too much noise! I believe that silence communicates more than speech. I like listening to the Jumna's waters, which speak to me in their own language.'

The Buddha was impressed by this boatman to whom the Jumna was a sort of deity with whom he conversed while ferrying his passengers from one bank to the other.

As the boat touched the other bank, and the passengers stepped out, the Buddha said to the boatman, 'I was delighted to be with you on both occasions. But what touched me most deeply was your resolve to give up liquor. You know, renunciation of any kind is the only way to salvation—not visiting temples and chanting slokas.'

It took him a couple of days to return to Kurukshetra where he'd promised to meet the tribal chiefs, Bhoollapati and Mullapati. Had they really sorted out all the problems that had brought them to the brink of a bloody fight? As he walked through the city to reach the tribal forest, he saw the tribals dancing and singing to drums. When he asked a tribal what it was all about, he learnt that it was an engagement ceremony between Bhoollapati's daughter,

Kopalya, and Mullapati's son, Subanni. So love had triumphed over hatred, the Buddha said to himself. He was happy to know that he'd arrived at an auspicious moment to witness a bond being forged between two sworn enemies. When the tribal chiefs saw the Buddha, they both came running up to him.

'We need your blessings, O Swamiji,' said Bhoollapati, 'for the young couple. You've indeed kept your word.'

'Well, it was ordained that I should be here to bless them.'

He was then introduced to the bridegroom and the bride.

'Both are skilled archers, Swamiji,' said Mullapati.

'But not as sharp shooters as myself,' the Buddha replied.

Recalling how the Buddha had displayed his skill with the bow, Mullapati said, 'Of course, nobody can excel you.'

There was a long pause after which the Buddha said, 'Why not renounce the bow as well, since it is a weapon of destruction? Why should there be any kind of violence?'

At this the young bridegroom interjected, 'Swamiji, it's the townsfolk who disturb our peace. They invade our land, hunting down our animals, cutting our trees for sandalwood . . . it's these poachers who provoke us into using our bows.'

The Buddha looked distraught over what he'd just heard.

'I do understand your problem,' he said, 'but I still feel that there should be a way to talk to these townsfolk.'

'When greed propels you, reasoning is of little avail, Swamiji,' said Bhoollapati.

'Maybe you could just scare them away with your bows and arrows,' said the Buddha, 'without shedding blood.'

'If only that was possible,' said Bhoollapati.

The Buddha was then invited to join the engagement feast at which a variety of food were served, but mostly meat dishes. The Buddha, however, helped himself only to some rice and milk.

Festivities over, the tribal chiefs requested a guest to let them drive the Buddha in their bullock cart, at least up to the outskirts of the forest.

Since he'd promised Ananda that he'd join him in Sarnath after his journey through this part of the country, he turned eastward. It turned out to be a long, arduous journey which took him a couple of months. Since his reputation as a spiritual leader followed him everywhere, he received warm hospitality in all the towns and villages that he passed through. It was mid-winter when he reached Kashi where he rested for a couple of days before moving on to Sarnath.

In Kashi, he faced stiff opposition from the local sadhus and pandits who felt that his teachings had challenged the very basis of their system which thrived on ritualism and the use of Sanskrit. On the other hand, the Buddha spoke in Pali and used homespun similes and metaphors that touched a deep chord in the common man.

When he entered Sarnath, he was given a tumultuous

welcome by Ananda and other followers. The first sermon that he had delivered here, a long time ago, still reverberated in the atmosphere—particularly his words that change and separation were the source of all pain, and that any man, regardless of birth, could attain nirvana, if he followed the Four Noble Truths and the eight-fold path to self-realization.

26

One morning, as the Buddha had finished his meditation, Ananda walked up to him and said, 'There is a royal messenger out there whose king, Pasenadi, wants to have an audience with you.'

'But you know that I don't give a appointments to anyone, king or beggar, because anybody can see me at any time.'

When Ananda said that Pasenadi was known to be a dreaded ruler who impaled his enemies, consigned them to solitary imprisonment or starved them to death, the Buddha looked interested. 'In that case, there's all the more reason that such a tyrant should be asked to cool his heels. Let him see me after my sermon this evening.'

That evening, the Buddha saw a silken-robed man sitting in the front row. He chose to speak on one of the aspects of his dharma—mindfulness.

'Today, I propose to explain the importance of one of the basic tenets of dharma. If a man wishes to attain divine bliss, he must feel concerned about the well-being of others, offer them compassion and understanding. The best way to empathize with the pain of fellow human beings is to imagine oneself in the same predicament. Let us prick a needle into our own finger to imagine the pain a man undergoes when he is impaled. Also, imagine yourself locked in a room, with all doors and windows shut, to visualize the plight of a prisoner in solitary confinement. You'd be relieved of your own pain if you consoled another person in distress.

'It is only through humility that one can climb up to the peak of divine bliss. We may learn from a ripened fruit how it bends its head, while a raw fruit perks up atop a tree cockily, unbending.'

Sermon over, the man in the silken robe walked up to the Buddha and said, 'O Lord, I am King Pasenadi of Kosala. Your sermon has awakened me to a new vision of life.'

The Buddha touched his right shoulder compassionately and said, 'I am very happy to meet you, and hear that you have learnt something from my discourse. You have my blessing for a happy and peaceful life.'

Then followed a brief silence during which the Buddha kept looking at the king who had the stern face of a hangman—eyes flashing with pride and anger, and dry hair spiked like a porcupine's bristles. But the Buddha observed that his stern countenance had now undergone a transformation. Was it an instant metamorphosis?

'May I ask a favour of you, O Lord?' the king asked in a voice, gentle and humble.

'Please . . .'

'Would you consider giving a sermon in Kosala? It would be an honour for me.'

'Indeed,' replied the Buddha. 'I'd be very pleased to do it.'

The next day, a chariot pulled up at the front gate of the monastery. When the Buddha arrived at the royal palace, King Pasenadi was himself there to receive him.

The Buddha was then taken to the royal reception hall which was luxuriously furnished—velvet sofas, gold-framed paintings on the walls, and a host of attendants standing all around. As the king sat next to the Buddha on a velvet sofa, an attendant walked in with a glass of fruit juice on a silver tray.

'This is from my mango grove,' the king said. 'In fact, if you are not too tired, I'd like to take you out for a ride through my Jeta grove.' Then, after a pause, he asked, 'Can you ride a horse?'

'I can try,' replied the Buddha, smiling.

When the king took him to his stable, the Buddha saw a host of horses. Pointing to a white horse, the king said, 'That's Julan, my favourite horse, fierce and temperamental. But I must get you a gentle animal—not the black mare under that peepal tree. She is a fire-breathing, savage creature.'

The Buddha flashed a smile and said, 'I'd like to ride that black mare, if you don't mind.'

Surprised, the king said, 'Are you sure, O Lord?'

'Absolutely,' came the prompt answer. As the Buddha drew close to the mare, she threatened to kick him off. But the Buddha's right hand had already started rippling down her mane, her flanks and the nape of her neck. Vanquished by this stranger's caressing, the mare let him mount her, without resisting.

'Amazing!' exclaimed Pasenadi. As they began riding through the grove, the king looked sideways at the Buddha who had set the mare into a gallop.

'I could never imagine a monk riding a savage animal with such skill.'

'Well, there are all kinds of monks . . .' the Buddha said, smiling again.

It was a vast grove, spanning about a dozen miles, with trees laden with ripe yellow mangoes, glistening in the mid-day sun. In the midst of every open space in the grove was a fountain, spurting jets of water into the air. The Buddha also saw some deer running about. A deer stopped in front of the Buddha, staring at this new visitor.

'A dream place,' said the Buddha.

'If you like this grove,' said the king, 'I'd be delighted to gift it to you. I have a couple of other groves . . . I'd also be pleased to set up a hermitage for you, near one of the fountains . . .'

'I am overwhelmed,' said the Buddha. Was this the man Ananda had described as a blood-thirsty tyrant? It seemed as if a brief sermon had struck milk out of a rock.

'I'd think about it,' said the Buddha. It was too much, too soon, he thought.

That evening, the Buddha chose a subject appropriate to the time and place—transformation.

'Every man,' he started off, 'can turn over a new leaf at some point or another. There is enough space in the human heart to open a new pathway. It's never too late to learn a new language, listen to a new voice or see a new star in the sky.' He paused. 'There are two kinds of deaths. If one kind is the extinction of the mortal frame, the other kind is our refusal to change and grow. Although human beings are enmeshed in a chain of becoming, a ceaseless flux, there are also moments of being and stillness. These are moments when we feel as if the boat of our soul is securely anchored—so stable and firm that not even a tempest can rock it.

'Don't forget that if sorrow is born of change and separation, release from pain is also possible if we follow the Dhammapada, the pathway to dharma.'

As a pall of silence descended over the place, the listeners felt as if a gentle breeze from the mango grove had rejuvenated the entire atmosphere. Discourse over, the king walked up to the dais, and bowed reverentially to him.

'Please don't . . .' the Buddha said, moved by the gesture.

'Why not?' said the king. 'If I am the king of Kosala, you

are the King of kings. And shouldn't a king make obeisance to his emperor?'

The Buddha hugged Pasenadi, warmly raising him to his feet.

'Would you take me as one of your disciples, O Lord?'

'It would be my pleasure,' responded the Buddha.

'What about the grove, a humble gift from your disciple?' the king asked.

'Yes, I'll gladly accept this wonderful gift,' replied the Buddha.

'I am delighted,' the king said. 'I'll now go ahead with setting up a hermitage for you. You may use it as your camp, away from the din of town life.' He paused. 'I hope this will be the beginning of a lasting bond between my guru and myself.'

'Between two friends,' countered the Buddha.

Thus was solemnized a bond of intimate friendship, that went on to span several years.

The Buddha now used this hermitage in the Jeta grove to relay directions to his favourite disciples Sariputta, Moggallana and, of course, Ananda whom he trusted most. They helped him not only in establishing the sangha but also propagating their master's teaching.

When the Buddha's message spread to most parts of the country, there was also stiff opposition from several quarters, particularly from Jains and Hindus.

But it was Devadatta who posed the greatest threat to

the sangha, which he plotted to disintegrate. His strategy was to induct himself into it as a monk and then engineer a revolt against the Buddha. Sensing his nefarious design, Ananda alerted his master against Devadatta.

Still, undeterred, the Buddha continued to travel and propagate his dharma. His main supporter was King Bimbisara of Magadha who, as his first royal patron, always offered him unstinted loyalty. No wonder the Buddha was heart-broken when he heard that he'd been forced to abdicate his throne in favour of his son, Ajatashatru, who not only held his father captive, but also starved him to death.

Whenever the Buddha returned to the Jeta grove, after his travels to new places, he used his time to relax. Here he spent some of his happiest days with Pasenadi who acted as his protector. As their intimacy grew, the Buddha began to advise him even about his diet. One day, when Pasenadi joined him over a meal in the hermitage, he noticed that the king ate like an ogre, gulping down platefuls of rice and drinking bowlfuls of milk.

'No, O King,' said the Buddha, 'this excessive eating can be very harmful. Pampering one's body is like lust, and it leads to all kinds of ailments.' This jolted Pasenadi into regulating his diet.

A week later, holding the Buddha's right hand in a fervent clasp, Pasenadi said, 'How I wish our bond of friendship could deepen into a blood relationship.' He paused. 'You know, I have so far never thought of marrying. If only you could find me a bride from your clan.'

The Buddha smiled on hearing the king's proposal.

'I'd indeed be delighted if such an alliance could come through.'

But by the time word reached Kapilavastu, the scenario there had changed. King Suddhodana had died and the Buddha's cousin, Mahanama, had assumed the reins of governance. Such a proposal provoked nothing but disdain and anger from the Sakya clan. Firstly, the Sakyas, jealous of the purity of their blood, would never let any of their girls marry an outsider and secondly, Pasenadi was hated in Kapilavastu as a tyrant king. Wasn't he the kind of man who would drive any woman to suicide? So, a conspiracy was hatched to pass on to King Pasenadi the illegitimate daughter, Vasabha, that Mahanama had sired through a slave-woman. She was sent to Pasenadi as a princess from the Sakya clan.

Since Vasabha was a beautiful women, with long black hair, eyes that glowed like a pair of moons, and a voice that was husky and seductive, King Pasenadi was charmed by her. She catapulted him into rapture in bed. Also, her affable manners won her the esteem of everyone in Kosala. When she gave birth to a son, there was jubilation all over the kingdom. The Buddha, too, was happy to see that through Vasabha, and her son, he could now claim to be a relation of Pasenadi—not knowing that his clan had trapped his friend into a fraudulent alliance.

The royal couple's son, Vidudabha, grew into a handsome prince, skilled in several martial arts—archery, hunting and horsemanship. But whenever it came to answering queries about his maternal ancestry, he would fob off all such questions. It was only when Vidudabha was seventeen that his mother let him visit Kapilavastu, together with a few soldiers. The party stayed at the royal guesthouse for a couple of days. But something happened that blew the lid off the plot that had been hatched by Mahanama. Just as Prince Vidudabha was ready to leave for Kosala, one of his soldiers, Vipula, said, 'Sir, I have forgotten my sword in the guesthouse. So would you, please, let me fetch it?'

'All right,' said the prince, 'but come back soon since we have a long ride ahead of us.'

'I'll be back in no time, sir.'

As he entered the guest house, he saw a woman, washing with milk the chair in which Vidudabha had sat. She was muttering something as she scrubbed the chair.

Here sat the prince,
son of my daughter,
once a slave-girl, but now a queen.
Let it all remain shrouded in mystery,

for even darkness cannot cover up the stains
that bare their teeth during sunlight.
Only milk can wipe off
what water cannot . . .

Mystified by her muttering, Vipula turned to her and asked, 'Who is this slave-girl, O woman? Is it Vasabha?'

The woman just stared blankly at the soldier, but did not utter a word. Then, brandishing his sword above her head, he shouted, 'I'll let your blood mingle with this milk if you don't speak out.'

Terrified, the woman stuttered, 'Yes.'

Vipula was stunned. He kept this secret from Prince Vidudabha but decided to report it all to King Pasenadi.

When Vipula told the king what he'd seen and heard in Kapilavastu, he exploded into a wild rage. With his eyes flashing, he bellowed like a wild bull. Turning to Vasabha and her son, he thundered, 'You rakshasas, I'll have you both impaled or roasted in an oven.'

Terrified, Vasabha stood leaning against a wall, while Vidudabha drew close to her as if to shield his mother. They looked like two rabbits dangling from a hunter's hands. So ear-piercing was Pasenadi's ranting that even the Buddha heard it, far away in his hermitage.

Then, turning to one of his attendants, the king said, 'Get me the Buddha here as well. I have something to ask him.'

But the Buddha was already up on his feet to walk over to the royal palace.

'O Lord,' the attendant said, 'the king wants you there immediately.'

As the Buddha entered the central hall, he saw the two helpless creatures standing against the wall, with a crowd of attendants and courtiers watching the scene. On seeing the Buddha, the king turned towards him.

'I guess that you knew how your cousin, Mahanama, has perpetrated a heinous fraud on me.'

Confounded, the Buddha responded, 'I don't know what you are talking about.'

'So you claim to be quite ignorant of how your cousin passed on to me Vasabha, a slave-woman, as a noble Sakya princess.'

Shocked, the Buddha said, 'I didn't have the faintest idea about all this. I believed that you'd married a Sakya princess. I am surprised and confounded.'

'I am amazed at your denial,' said Pasenadi, raising his voice to a high pitch. 'So you didn't know how your clan has cheated me.'

Realizing what had happened, the Buddha said, 'In the first place I no longer belong to the Sakya clan, because my family is now all of humanity. Secondly, I don't recognize any difference between a king and a slave, because birth is only an accident. Finally, what sin has Vidudabha committed to be disowned and punished by you? Doesn't your blood now run in his veins?'

There was something in the Buddha's words that made the king pause.

'But don't you see how I have lived,' said the king, 'in the dark all these sixteen years?'

'I do understand your predicament,' said the Buddha. 'But hasn't Vasabha served you dutifully and faithfully all these years? It would be a gross injustice if you impaled them.' He paused. 'It seems you have lapsed into your old self . . .'

'Well, I may have many selves,' jibed the king, 'but I propose to teach this woman and her son a bitter lesson . . . And, as for you, O Buddha, I request you to leave my grove immediately for what your clan has done to me, whether you were privy to this treachery or not.'

'As you wish, O King,' said the Buddha. 'I am a wandering monk and the entire country is open to me.'

While the Buddha prepared to leave for Sarnath the next morning, he heard that the king had ordered both Vasobha and Vidudabha to be stripped of their royal positions, tonsured and sent out of Kosala.

In Sarnath, the Buddha remained sunk in depression for a few days, for leaving the Jeta grove. It was like going into exile. But since suffering had been his lot, he took it all stoically. He told Ananda that he had left the grove to be with the sangha.

One morning, when he was with Sariputta, Moggallana

and Ananda, he was pleasantly surprised to learn that Ananda had an incredible memory.

'You know, O Lord,' said Moggallana, 'that on the tablet of his memory is etched every word you have spoken in your sermons.'

Touching Ananda's head affectionately, the Buddha said, 'Then his memory will be my successor, not any monk.'

One morning, after the Buddha had finished his meditation, Ananda said, 'O Lord, may I ask you something that has been troubling the minds of many monks?'

'Yes, go ahead,' he replied.

'How should one interact with women, O Master?'

'Try to keep your eyes off them,' pat came the response.

'But how should one act if seeing them becomes inevitable?' Ananda pressed on.

'Don't engage yourself in any conversation with them, because you may then get involved.'

Not satisfied with this answer, Ananda continued, 'What if one finds oneself conversing with them?'

'Then be mindful,' the Buddha responded, 'because, finally, it is your mind that will show you the way out.'

One day when Ananda and Moggallana were at a grocery store, purchasing provisions for the monastery, they were surrounded by a group of Jains who began to hurl abuses at them.

'You monks have descended upon this city like locusts to destroy it,' sneered a tall, stocky Jain.

While Ananda remained silent, Moggallana couldn't help retaliating. 'While you Jains preach non-violence, you use your tongues as a sword . . . Is that what you have learnt from your guru, Lord Mahavira?'

When one of the Jains leapt at Moggallana's throat and was about to strangle him, Ananda intervened, saying, 'Let me apologize to you on his behalf. Our master wouldn't have approved of retaliation in any form.'

Although Ananda's words calmed the Jains, one of them still continued to shout. 'I'll take care of him one of these days . . . your dharma is fake, and you are all imposters.'

Ananda held Moggallana's arm and walked him away, whispering into his ears, 'You can't argue with mad people. Let's go.'

A week later something happened that shattered the monastery. It was a dark night, with no moon or stars. But since a cool breeze was blowing, Moggallana chose to sleep out in the front yard. At the stroke of midnight, a masked man jumped over the compound wall, plunged his knife into Moggallana's heart and bolted away. Hearing the commotion all the monks rushed out and they saw Moggallana lying dead in a pool of blood.

When the Buddha learnt how one of his favourite disciples had been murdered, he was shocked. 'There has fallen one of my main props,' he said to himself, tears flowing from his eyes.

But little did the Buddha know that he'd soon face

another blow. A week later, it was Sariputta's turn. He was poisoned by a Brahmin who felt that his priesthood was threatened by the Buddha's teachings. One morning, as Sariputta had finished his meditation, the Brahmin offered him a glass of milk, saying, 'This is as pure as divine nectar, O monk.'

But just as Sariputta took a couple of sips, he felt dizzy and fell to the ground. Before the monks could reach the spot, the Brahmin had vanished from the scene.

The Buddha took Sariputta's death as another blow. 'When misfortunes come,' he said to himself, 'they never fall like driblets, but like a downpour.'

The last few months of his life turned out to be very agonizing. With dissensions brewing in the sangha, he saw it almost on the verge of disintegration. It was only Ananda who assiduously tried to hold the fraternity together. He never lost faith in his master's dharma which, he firmly believed, was the only panacea for the world's malaise.

The Buddha was now left with only one close disciple, Ananda, who followed him everywhere like his shadow. If something happened to him, he thought, it would be the end of Buddhism, because in his memory was stored his entire teaching.

27

One day, the Buddha sprang a surprise on Ananda, saying that he'd like to give a discourse, on death. So would he send word about it all round?

'But your body is now very fragile, O Master, and your feet . . .' he trailed off.

'No, Ananda,' the Buddha said, 'I have enough strength to speak for an hour or so. When the spirit is willing, the body must cooperate. There are occasions when one speaks from the heart, not the tongue.'

Ananda felt that he had no choice but to obey him.

It was a large crowd that gathered in Sarnath's central park. Everyone saw a fragile figure climbing up to the dais. Then, as silence descended all over the place, the Buddha started in a voice that sounded like a broken reed. Although his legs and hands were shaking, his eyes glowed with the Divine Light.

'This may be my last sermon, for hereafter I propose only to meditate, not speak. This evening, I intend sharing with you my thoughts on a subject that has recently occupied my mind—death. Death is the finalé to our existence on the earth. Anything that has a beginning must have an end. But we need not be fearful of death, because it opens a portal to another life. Remember that the man who has just died is also the man who is born elsewhere.

'Let us never forget that change and separation are the cardinal facts of life. The only thing that is immutable is the soul. It has no end because it has no beginning. It is imperishable because fire cannot burn it, nor water wet it. It resides in the body until its extinction when it flies into the cosmos. There it stays for a few days, before it enters a new body. So it is the spirit that keeps the cycle of birth and death moving, forever. As regards human beings, they remain embroiled in a process of flux, like a river that never stops flowing. We never dip our feet into the same stream twice because the waters have flowed on.

'So, if death is inevitable, how can we come to terms with it? The only way to face it fearlessly is to subjugate our desires, and live truthfully and meaningfully. Only then will we be able to face Yama with a smile on our face. The truth about a man's real identity becomes manifest only from his thoughts on his deathbed. Does he still think of what he is leaving behind—his wealth and family? Then he must feel the pangs of deprivation and separation. What peace can such a man's soul attain in the life beyond?

'Let me now say a word about different forms of death. There is a death that comes after prolonged illness, spanning several months or even years. Then there is a death that comes like a boon during one's sleep, a quiet painless release from life's sorrows and miseries.

'The moment of death can also be the time for introspection, for as we take our last breath we may see, in our mind's eye, all our past deeds flashing past as a pageant. It all depends on the baggage of good or evil deeds that a soul carries with it when it departs from the body. On one's karma, therefore, depends the nature of one's re-birth.'

The Buddha then suddenly started coughing as if he'd run out of breath. At once, Ananda brought him a glass of water. After taking a few sips, he resumed.

'The real source of pain is the fact that we are trapped in a cycle of birth and death. Our life is like a whirlpool in which we get hurtled from one side to the other, caught in dark swirling waters. Or, it is like a see-saw, with death at one end and birth at the other. Rebirth, as I've said, is itself a form of punishment, for human existence and sorrow are coterminous. We are born in our mother's pain and we die in our own.

'Of course, rebirth as a human being is a blessing, because one may be reborn as a bullock, sweating and groaning under the yoke all its life. Or, as a snake crawling on its belly, seeking refuge from danger in a bush or a hole.

'So we return to the problem of pain, release from which is possible only through following the Four Noble Truths and the eight-fold path to divine bliss. Nirvana is not only for monks because any man, Brahmin or Shudra, can achieve it through disengagement from worldly attachments. For such a man, there will be only one death and no more. No more suffering, no disease and no deprivation.'

His voice now suddenly became very hoarse, almost inaudible. As he raised his hands to bless the listeners, everyone surged forward to touch his feet. The Buddha then placed his left hand on Ananda's right shoulder to help himself step down from the dais. As Ananda was taking him away, a man walked up to the Buddha. He was in his mid-forties. His complexion was ashen-grey. In the middle of his head was a patch of baldness. His nose was hooked like a parrot's. Ananda noticed something asymmetrical about him, because while his left ear seemed to be a little larger than his right ear, his upper lip was thicker than the lower one. In his voice was a stutter as if he wasn't certain of what he wanted to say.

'O Lord,' he stuttered, 'may I p . . . l . . . e . . . ase ask a favour of you? Would you bless my house with your presence?' He paused as if he wasn't sure how to say the next request. 'And would you have a meal with me?' He then added, 'I am a silversmith and my name is Cinha.'

Since there was a ring of expectancy in his voice, the Buddha nodded his head.

After he left, Ananda turned to the Buddha and said, 'O Master, why did you agree to dine at his house? Somehow, I didn't like that man—I mean the look in his eyes.'

'No, Ananda,' said the Buddha. 'Didn't his request sound like a supplication?'

'Can I also come along with you?' said Ananda.

'Of course,' said the Buddha. 'You know that I want you with me everywhere, all the time.'

It was a house, with a panelled door on which his name 'Cinha' was engraved. As the Buddha and Ananda were asked to sit on a mat, the man went inside to ask his wife to get the meal ready. A little later, Cinha spread a plantain leaf on which he laid out something that looked unidentifiable. Was it meat or some vegetable? the Buddha wondered. When it emitted a strange odour, the Buddha was perplexed. But since he'd never refused any kind of food served to him, he decided to eat it. When Cinha returned with some rice and milk, the Buddha said to him, 'O friend, I'll eat what you brought me earlier, but let my companion have only rice and milk.'

When the man went inside again, presumably to bring water or fruit, Ananda asked the Buddha, 'Why don't you let me also eat what was served to you earlier? I'm confused . . .'

With an enigmatic smile, the Buddha replied, 'You are now the entire world to me, Ananda. If something happens to you, it would be a disaster.'

As the Buddha took a morsel of the food, he felt a strange sensation in his stomach. Then he gathered himself up to go out. But when he threw up, Ananda was alarmed.

'You don't look too well, O Master,' he said. 'I'm worried.'

'I'm all right,' the Buddha responded. When his host returned, he asked him to dig a deep pit and bury the leftovers of the food he'd just eaten.

'But there was nothing wrong with the food, O Lord,' Cinha said. 'My wife had cooked something special for you . . .'

'I know,' said the Buddha, 'and I wish to thank you and your wife for your hospitality.'

As he vomited again, Ananda held him by his right arm and led him away. Boiling with anger, he asked him, 'Why did he serve you that food?'

'No, Ananda, let's not think unkindly of him . . . maybe he meant well.'

'Your impulsion to forgive is irrepressible,' Ananda said, somewhat irritably.

That night the Buddha kept tossing about restlessly. Nor did Ananda have a wink of sleep. All night, he stood anxiously at the door, watching his master groaning. When dawn broke, the Buddha called him, 'Why are you so worried? Don't you remember what I said in my last sermon? Maybe my time has come, and I am ready to go.'

Sobbing, Ananda said, 'I wouldn't let you . . .'

'Can anyone escape death, Ananda?'

'I am not in a mood to hear you say all this,' said Ananda, and he looked away to hide his tears.

'Don't be too anxious, my dear,' the Buddha tried to console his favourite disciple. Maybe I could still muster enough strength to stay on a little longer.' He paused. 'Since I don't want any public mourning over my death, let us clear out of Pava. I wish to close my eyes in some nondescript place—some small, unknown village.'

'As you wish,' answered Ananda, dolefully.

Outside, the sunrise remained veiled behind a cluster of dark clouds. There was now a haze all around, and a chilly wind started howling.

The Buddha then spoke in a feeble voice. 'How about going to Kushmara?'

'But that's about four miles away.'

'I think I'll be able to make it, Ananda.'

28

Surprisingly, the Buddha picked up enough strength to set out on what was destined to be the last lap of his journey. He somehow managed to walk till Kushmara, the place he'd chosen for his final rest.

Ananda couldn't help but feel concerned for his master. His heart bled to see him trudging along the road, coughing and sighing. Occasionally, he stopped to lean against some wayside tree to recover his breath. So indomitable was his spirit that he walked on as steadily as possible. But whenever he stumbled, Ananda rushed forward to help him to his feet.

'O Master, I can't bear to see you suffering so much . . . I feel scared.'

'My body, dear Ananda, is now a crumbling mud-house which cannot withstand any longer the ravages of time. Let its walls and roof collapse . . . don't worry about me, my dear . . . maybe I have overstayed on this earth.'

'Please don't say that,' muttered Ananda. 'We'd feel orphaned without you.'

'There you go again. I reiterate that when I'm gone, let my teachings stay with you as your friend and guide.'

As they resumed their walking, Ananda drew close to his master, and whispered into his ears, fearfully, 'There's a tiger following us.'

The Buddha looked back and saw a huge tiger, its striped body glistening in the mid-day sun. Its hazel-green eyes were focused on the two human beings walking ahead of it.

'I'm scared,' said Ananda, in a tremulous voice.

'Why be afraid?' said the Buddha. 'Maybe this animal is out seeking something—food or shelter in this hot sun . . . no, it wouldn't harm us if we don't look at it threateningly. Let it walk behind us, as a fellow-traveller.'

They had just gone a little distance further when Ananda said, 'It's vanished, Master, somewhere in the bushes to our left.'

'I told you so,' said the Buddha. 'These animals also follow their own dharma—peace, tolerance and compassion.'

They were about to reach the outskirts of Kushmara when the Buddha began to show signs of acute pain and fatigue.

'I'm feeling thirsty,' he said. 'Take my bowl and get me some water.'

Although Ananda spotted a stream a little distance away, he returned without water.

'I saw a shallow stream,' he told the Buddha, 'but its water looked turbid and muddy . . . it seems that some carts had rolled through it, making its water undrinkable.'

Ananda then hurried away again to look for water elsewhere. This time he spotted a pool full of crystal clear water. He rushed back to the Buddha with a bowlful of this water. Drinking it, he felt rejuvenated. The Buddha was now able to walk up to the pool himself to have his bath. When he stepped out, Ananda noticed, for the first time, thirty-two marks on his body—signs of his divinity.

Resuming their walk, they crossed the river Hirannavate and entered Kushmara. Fortunately, the first house they knocked at offered them food and rest. When their host learnt that his guest was none else but the Buddha, he felt that the gods had blessed his house.

As the Buddha now lay in a bed, he said to Ananda, 'Looks like this is the end.'

Ananda was terrified at the thought of losing his master. Crying, he said, 'O Lord, don't forsake me.'

'There you go again, worrying about my body's extinction. This is a denial of whatever I've taught you so far—that the mortal frame is only a vesture for the spirit.' He paused. 'So, as my worthiest disciple, arrange for me to lie on the ground with my head facing the north.'

The Buddha then lay on a sheet spread on the ground, and assumed the posture of a lion, turning onto his right side.

Then, with tears streaming down his cheeks, Ananda asked him if he'd like to give any specific directions for his last rites.

'Just give me an ordinary cremation,' he said in a feeble voice, 'and let my ashes be scattered over a paddy field.'

After saying this, he closed his eyes and sank into silence. Had he gone into a trance? Ananda wondered. But since he saw his lips moving, he thought the Buddha was perhaps communicating with a spirit. Quietly, he stood at the door, his eyes riveted on his face.

Suddenly, the Buddha saw a dark figure standing in front of him. It was a squint-eyed, stocky man with very long hands that looked like the claws of a raven. 'I hope you have recognized me,' the man said.

'Yama!' the Buddha exclaimed.

'I knew you'd recognize me instantly.'

'I do feel privileged, O Buddha,' the man said, 'to be asked to escort you to *svarga*, for that's where you belong. Ordinarily, I meet individuals who are bound to the wheel of birth and death. But, in your case, I know it will be my last meeting with you, for you have attained nirvana—no more birth or death for you.'

The Buddha flashed a smile.

'Do you still feel any pain after eating that meal?' Yama asked. 'You know, it was ordained that you'd be served that food, for how else would I have come here to meet you?'

'I've already asked Ananda,' said the Buddha, 'not to

blame Cinha.' He paused. 'So I'm now ready to embark on a new voyage with you . . . but would you, please, spare a little time for me as I have a few questions for you?'

'All the time you need,' he responded promptly, 'although I'm always very hard pressed for time. This is because countless people are dying at every moment. Since I don't have any time to talk to individuals, I sometimes organize multiple deaths through earthquakes, shipwrecks, riots . . . but let me tell you that I have a fantastic memory for names.'

'Amazing!' exclaimed the Buddha. Then, after a pause, he asked, 'Since plague may also be one of your instruments of annihilation, would you remember Dharmi of Greha?'

'Oh, that prostitute,' Yama replied. 'An extraordinary woman! You may not know that she died soon after you left Greha. Her last thoughts were of you, because she'd fallen deeply in love with you. Poor thing, she didn't know that you were on your way to nirvana.'

The Buddha was saddened to hear about Dharmi's death.

'Where did you take her?' the Buddha asked, anxiously.

'To *svarga*, of course, for that's where she belonged.'

There was a brief pause after which the Buddha asked, 'And what about my Kanaka?'

'I know Channa has already told you that he buried him on the bank of the Satya, precisely where you parted from him. Well, he too attained nirvana, because his dedication to you was far deeper than anybody else's.'

The Buddha heaved a deep sigh. 'My only regret was that

he couldn't speak, but he always communicated with me through gestures—snorts, tears and sighs.' A pause. 'I have also often thought of a tortoise I knew in Uruvala. There was so much I learnt from it—self-restraint, slow but steady steps along the pathway of life, and deep meditation. To me it was an icon of wisdom.'

'It's still there, living by that pond,' said Yama. 'Incidentally, its name is Guruvesh. It belongs to a clan that can live up to six hundred years or so . . . Let me tell you that one of its great-great-grandfathers fought in the battle of Kurukshetra, as the deputy commander of a division in the Pandava army.'

'Illustrious lineage!' exclaimed the Buddha.

'I, too, have a special regard for the tortoise species,' said Yama, 'because I don't have to seize any of them too often. On the other hand, it can be quite boring, you know, to meet the same human soul every sixty or seventy years. It's, of course, agonizing to seize a child at the delivery itself. But, in a sense, it also salvages it from the travails of human existence—disease, betrayal, poverty and what not.'

Finding Yama's observations on life both amusing and enlightening, the Buddha asked him about the sadhu he'd met on the cremation ground.

'Oh, that sadhu . . . but asceticism, I tell you, is no way to attain self-realization. That man, I know, lived under my shadow all the time, drinking water from a skull, and hardly eating anything. Wasn't he trying to invite me much before his time? So I had to oblige him. I got him just a year after you left him . . . incidentally, when you were looking for him during your journey homeward, his skull lay right there on top of a heap of skulls.'

'One last question, please, O Prince of Darkness,' said the Buddha, 'although I'm aware that I have held you far too long.'

'Never mind,' said Yama. 'Go ahead. It's been a great pleasure talking to you.'

'Channa has been uppermost in my mind for quite some time. May I know if he is alive or dead?'

'He's still there,' replied Yama. 'The only thing that keeps him going is the memory of you. He is now ninety but he can still drive a chariot.'

The Buddha's eyes brightened. 'How I wish I could meet him before I'm taken away.'

'That may not be possible, I'm afraid, for it's now time for me to carry you away to heaven.'

'I'm ready. Nothing to pack up. You know that I've always travelled light, with just a saffron robe and a brass bowl.'

'I know that,' Yama said. 'But let me tell you my experience with Pharaoh Ramesses II. When I went to seize him, he began to cry bitterly like a child, terrified by death. He also wanted to take his chest of treasure with him—diamonds, rubies and gold. When I told him that he would have to leave everything behind, he wanted to have his chest placed beside his body in the grave. Stupid man!'

'Interesting, said the Buddha. 'It's pathetic to see human beings caught in the grip of greed, even on their death bed.' He paused. Then he asked, 'What was the status of his re-birth?'

'He was reborn as a petty silversmith in a small village, down the valley of the Nile.'

The Buddha smiled.

Conversation over, Yama drew close to the Buddha and closed his eyes, tenderly and compassionately. As Ananda then heard his master's throat rattle, he understood that he was gone. He began to cry and many people appeared on the scene.

Tears streaming down his cheeks, Ananda carried the Buddha's body and laid it on the ground, in the front yard. Everyone saw a new star appearing in the sky, brighter than any other star around.

A little before the cremation, everyone witnessed a strange phenomenon. Although it was not springtime, withered flowers from the sal trees suddenly blossomed and began to fall over the Buddha's body, covering it like a floral sheet. From the sky dropped sandalwood powder, which lent a pleasant aroma to the atmosphere. Then, a melody reverberated in the air as if the earth and the sky were singing a duet.

Tearfully, Ananda now arranged a pyre on which he placed his master's body. Surprisingly, before he could light the fire, the pyre erupted into flames by itself. He then recited a few lines from the Buddha's favourite verse:

> O architect of the mud-house
> now that I have seen thee,
> never again shall I let you build these walls
> of suffering, nor nurture this lofty tree
> of falsehood, nor raise new columns
> on the clay. Demolished is this house,
> its columns fractured—all designed by deception.
> Now I shall voyage forward to my ultimate goal . . .
> Nirvana!

A NOTE ON THE AUTHOR

Shiv K. Kumar has donned many hats and lived many lives: poet, novelist, short-story writer, playwright, translator, academic and critic. He was born in Lahore, where he received his school and college education. He obtained his doctorate in English literature from the University of Cambridge. Professor Kumar has published thirteen volumes of poetry, five novels, two collections of short stories and a play. His poems have appeared in several renowned newspapers and journals including the *New York Times*, *Poetry Review* (London), and *Western Humanities Review*—and been broadcast on the BBC. In 1978, he was elected a Fellow of the Royal Society of Literature (London). He received the Sahitya Akademi Award in 1987 for his collection of poems *Trapfalls in the Sky*. In 2001, he was awarded the Padma Bhushan for his contribution to literature.

ACKNOWLEDGEMENTS

I am deeply indebted to Fazal Rashid, assistant editor, Vintage Books, for his invaluable editorial inputs, Shalaja Rao for improving the manuscript in many ways, and Vandana who encouraged me to write this book.